PERFECT TAROT
DIVINATION

PERFECT TAROT DIVINATION

Through Astrology,
Kabbalah, and Principles of
Jungian Interpretation

Robert Wang

VOLUME III
The Jungian Tarot Trilogy
PRACTICAL STUDIES

Marcus Aurelius Press

Acknowledgments

Sincere thanks are due Judith Hawkins-Tillirson for her insightful review of the manuscript and for her recommendations on several key points of astrology. Thanks are also due to Vincent Messina for his criticism of this book at an early stage and for his suggestions about approaching astrology from the standpoint of "unusual" situations, and to the late Matthew Tapper, who tested this system over a period of several years, as it was being developed, and found that it yielded unusually accurate results.

CONTENTS

The Jungian Tarot, one of the most unique tarot decks ever created, is the product of five years of intensive research. The cards, painted in oil on canvas, were produced in consultation with practicing clinical psychologists and with Jungian analysts at the C.G. Jung Institutes in Zurich and in New York. Some unique ideas for the integration of Jungian concepts into this visual format were provided by academic specialists in comparative religion, who pointed out ways in which an archetypal theme appears under different cultural guises, some of which are little known. By example one may cite the white horse found in the card of *Death*, an image understood by Jungians to relate to the Great Mother. And every symbolic image in the cards has a very special meaning in relation to one or more of the archetypes. The most general symbol in each of the Trump cards is the Mandala, the perfect circle which Carl Jung considered to be the self under a variety of conditions.

Tarot, which developed as a game in the fourteenth century and which by the seventeenth century had been turned into a device for telling fortunes, has never been a unified study. The cards, which originally represented the world of courtly medieval pleasures, have been assigned a wide variety of mutually exclusive divinatory meanings which are a source of confusion to many.

Perfect Tarot Divination is a book intended for anyone who has been uncomfortable with the completely arbitrary way in which, over the centuries, attributions of meanings have been attached to the cards. Clearly, there are no absolutes in tarot interpretation, which is the reason that so many different systems "work." A divination depends, subconsciously and unconsciously, upon the meanings that a reader has assigned to each card and the consistent application of these meanings. There is no absolutely correct way to interpret the cards, but tradition states that the closer a system of attributions is to a pattern of inner "truth," the better, and a method of divination related to the Kabbalistic "Tree of Life" (see appendix) seems ideal in this regard. Here may be the explanation of the fact that most who use the Jungian Tarot cards (developed to reflect archetypal interactions) in conjunction with a system of attributions which are pure astrology, report a very remarkable degree of accuracy in readings.

The unique advantage of the Jungian Tarot method is in the complexity of relationships which it demonstrates. The technique shows not only an event, but the root causes of that event (from a number of different directions) and provides information for the reader not available with other systems.

Another point which might be made here is that many teachers of these subjects explain that the real significance of tarot divination is not predicting the future, but is the development of individual psychic abilities.

Whatever may be the aim, of the reader, it will be obvious that a very complicated system is presented here, one demanding serious commitment. But those who are already expert in astrology will be pleasantly surprised to find that they are able to immediately interpret The Jungian Tarot cards with considerable depth. It should, however, be understood that divination with these cards is only one part of a program intended to be applied at three levels: The first level is spiritual, applying techniques of meditation and regression into self-exploration, as well as Jungian analysis with archetypal images. The second level is intellectual, a historical and visual introduction to Jungian psychology. And the third level is practical, the use of the cards for divination.

While this small book, *Perfect Tarot Divination,* provides a comprehensive system for divination, another book, *Tarot Psychology* is an introduction to the complex symbolism of the cards and provides a self-study method for what Jung called "active imagination" with the archetypal images of the cards. A third book, *The Jungian Tarot and its Archetypal Imagery*, considers both the historical development of the cards, and archetypes, such as the "Great Mother" or the "Hero Son" as they are encountered in a variety of religious systems and as they may be encountered in personal meditational use.

A General Note On Attributions

These meanings are derived by attributing a full ten planets to the Kabbalistic Tree of Life, including Pluto as Kether, Uranus as Chokmah, Neptune as Binah, and Saturn as Malkuth. Ten planets in this tarot scheme allows for a seamless and logical mesh of Kabbalistic principles with astrological meanings traditionally given for Planets and for their interaction with the Signs of the Zodiac.

A note should also be made about the Court Cards. As a general rule the Kings and Queens represent real persons who are in some way involved with the person in question. The Princes and the Princesses usually are a point of view or a behavior. For example, *The King of Wands* might represent a real executive in a company. If, the King were linked with *The Prince of Swords* in a very negative way, it could suggest that the King were becoming mentally ill or losing touch with reality. If *The Prince of Swords* were to appear alone in a cell, and well-placed, it would mean rather gentle and intelligent behavior and a tendency to escape into a mental world, probably on the part of the person who is the subject of the divination. What is important here is that the behavior of the four Kings and the four Queens, the real people, is not limited to the ways in which they are described in the following sections.

To begin, the cards are shuffled in whatever way is comfortable and fifteen cards are spread out in five "cells" according to the following scheme:

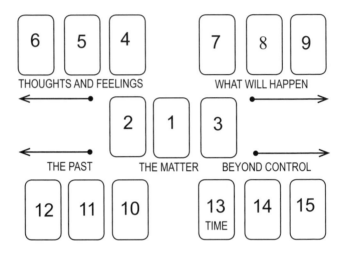

One of the most interesting and useful features of this spread is that after introducing the question as the center cell of three cards, and after showing the overt developments in the upper right cell, the covert thoughts and feelings affecting the matter are clearly shown in the upper left cell.

ONE, TWO, THREE: *The Matter*. Card one, read first, is central and is modified by cards two and three. The cards show the situation as it is. Here a court cart which resembles the person in question may appear. In any event, the experienced reader will immediately see a relationship between these cards and the cards of other cells.

FOUR, FIVE, SIX: *Thoughts and Feelings*. These cards often show hidden thoughts and feelings that will cause what will appear in the next three cards. It is not unusual that this cell defines unconscious materials, such as repressed hostilities (or even affections) unrecognized by the person about whom the reading is being given. Hidden dangers will also appear in this section.

SEVEN, EIGHT, NINE: *What Will Happen*. This is what is going to happen, and what will be evident and obvious. A key part of the reading is to understand how these cards came about. They may be the result of an interaction of the energies of the other three cells, or of only one. Perhaps the future events are completely out of the control of the person in question. Or perhaps they are being brought about by secret plots and thoughts shown in cards four, five, and six.

TEN, ELEVEN, TWELVE: *The Past*. These cards show what has happened in the past that may now be affecting the present.

THIRTEEN, FOURTEEN, FIFTEEN: *Beyond Control*. The Three final cards show forces at work (which may not always be obvious) about which a person can do nothing.

Up to three additional cards may, if desired, be placed upon any given card, to amplify and explain its meaning. Thus, minimally, this spread requires fifteen cards, but it may use as many as forty-five.

A point which must be made is that this process of divination is intuitive, and a truly excellent reader will occasionally go with feelings which may run against the grain of any of the structure presented here. There is an interesting psychic key, as experience demonstrates, which is that the reader has to "go with the flow," put his or her own ego aside, and say whatever comes to mind before rational processes can edit the materials. It is very important to be willing to be wrong.

Sequence of Time

Information about the time framework involved in a reading is, quite logically, to be found in the lower right-hand section which shows things beyond the control of the person in question.

Time framework is given by card number thirteen and is shown by the suit of the card in that position. If the card is a Trump, something is happening at the moment. A sequence of time is shown by the Wands (very fast) through the Pentacles (very slow). The principle is based on the Four Worlds of the Kabbalah. Wands represent pure spirit and thus rapid acting; Cups are the collective unconscious and are somewhat fast; Swords are conscious thought, which is moderately paced, compared to the above forms of consciousness; and Pentacles are the Earth, which is slow and plodding. Thus, the following is established:

> A Trump=Something is happening now.
> A Wand=Something will happen in days.
> A Cup=Something will happen in weeks.
> A Sword=Something will happen in months.
> A Pentacle=Something will happen
> in a year or more.

Basic Principles

The following materials may, at first, appear inordinately complicated. But they are arranged so that, as opposed to other tarot systems, there can be absolutely no doubt about the origins of each and every attribution of meaning to a card. The most important materials have been summed-up as "Keys" and should be committed to memory. The more complicated of the attributions can be referenced as needed, and eventually what must at first appear to be an insanely disparate set of thoughts will become not only very clear, but very comfortable.

The system of tarot divination is based entirely upon accepted principles of traditional astrology which, for the first time, brings tarot interpretation into a three thousand year old divinatory mainstream. What is involved is essentially translating the language of astrology into the pictures of the tarot. For example, once it has been determined that *The Empress* is Venus, it is understood that anything which traditional astrology says about Venus can be said about the card: Venus is an Earthy energy which rules the signs Taurus and Libra. So there is a special relationship between *The Empress*, *The Hierophant*, and *Justice*. When, in tarot, such emphasis is placed on the Four Elements, i.e., Fire, Water, Air, and Earth, it can be stated simply that:

All Wands are Fire.
All Cups are Water.
All Swords are Air.
All Pentacles are Earth.

The Zodiac Opposites

The system of tarot opposites in the cards of the Zodiac is explained by the scheme: Aries (*Emperor*, Fire) is the opposite of Libra (*Justice*, Air); Taurus (*Hierophant*, Earth) is the opposite of Scorpio (*Death*, Water); Gemini (*Lover*, Air) is the opposite of Sagittarius (*Temperance*, Fire); Cancer (*Hanged Man*, Water) is the opposite of Capricorn (*Devil*, Earth); Leo (*Strength*, Fire) is the opposite of Aquarius (*Star*, Air); Virgo (*Hermit*, Earth) is the opposite of Pisces (*Judgment*, Water). For tarot divination this astrological scheme for the Signs of the Zodiac breaks down to a simple and easily remembered chart of oppositions.

Key One: Tarot Oppositions
(Increased effect of both: they stimulate each other)

EMPEROR (Aries) opposite to JUSTICE (Libra)
HIEROPHANT (Taurus) opposite to DEATH (Scorpio)
LOVER (Gemini) opposite to TEMPERANCE (Sagittarius)
HANGED MAN (Cancer) opposite to DEVIL (Capricorn)
STRENGTH (Leo) opposite to STAR (Aquarius)
HERMIT (Virgo) opposite to JUDGMENT (Pisces)

Key Two: Rulerships

THE FOOL rules DEATH and THE ACES.

THE MAGICIAN rules THE STAR and THE TWOS.

THE HIGH PRIESTESS rules JUDGMENT and THE THREES.

THE WHEEL OF FORTUNE rules TEMPERANCE and THE FOURS.

THE TOWER rules THE EMPEROR and THE FIVES.

THE SUN rules STRENGTH and THE SIXES.

THE EMPRESS rules THE HIEROPHANT, JUSTICE, and THE SEVENS.

THE CHARIOT rules THE LOVER, THE HERMIT, and THE EIGHTS.

THE MOON rules THE HANGED MAN and THE NINES.

THE WORLD rules THE DEVIL and THE TENS.

Key Three: Elemental Affinities of Planets

MAGICIAN, Uranus. Airy.
HIGH PRIESTESS, Neptune. Watery.
EMPRESS, Venus. Earthy.
CHARIOT, Mercury. Airy.
WHEEL OF FORTUNE, Jupiter. Watery.

TOWER, Mars. Fiery.
MOON, Moon. Watery.
SUN, Sun. Fiery.
WORLD, Saturn. Earthy.

A TECHNICAL NOTE FOR VERY ADVANCED READERS: *Although the assignment of elements to planets has varied widely among different systems, it is clear that the architects of the Hermetic Kabbalah wanted us to understand that the elemental affinities of planets are a moveable feast dependent upon the qualities of the Four Worlds (Atziluth=Spirit, Briah=Mind, Yetzirah=Imagination and Assiah=Matter) in which they are operating. This seems to have been one of the deep practical secrets of the system, although few people would have any idea how to use this information, which has special significance for ritual.*

In that remarkable compendium of Kabbalistic correspondences, 777, the relationship of elements to planets on the Tree of Life is as follows: 1) Kether, The Root of Air, 2) Chokmah, The Root of Fire, 3) Binah, The Root of Water, 4) Chesed, Water, 5) Geburah, Fire, 6) Tiphareth, Air, 7) Netzach, Fire, 8) Hod, Water, 9) Yesod, Air, and 10) Earth. For astrologers considering the Sephiroth as planetary forces, the scheme may appear to make little sense until it is understood that this perfect balance of Air, Fire, and Water is specific to the Spiritual World—Atziluth.

However, the "Working Tree" of tarot and of meditation uses the Paths of Atziluth and the Sephiroth of Briah, the Mental World of "formation." In Briah, elemental forces, as they apply within each planetary "realm," are represented with great simplicity by colors. Thus, using the modern system of planets on the Tree of Life, the following elements are appropriately applied:

1) Kether/Pluto: White/root of the Elements
2) Chokmah/Uranus: Grey/Air
3) Binah/Neptune: Black/Water
4) Chesed/Jupiter: Blue/Water
5) Geburah/Mars: Red/Fire
6) Tiphareth/Sun: Yellow/Fire
7) Netzach/Venus: Green/ Earth
8) Hod/ Mercury: Orange/Air
9) Yesod/ Moon: Purple/Water
10) Malkuth/Saturn: Citrine, Olive, Yellow, Black/ Earth

The Hermetic Kabbalistic color assignments of the two Lower Worlds would suggest that elemental energies are so variable in each of the planetary Sephiroth that they may change as the environment in which they exist is changed, either through imagination (Yetzirah) or through physical movement (Assiah).

Beyond the obvious fact that cards of the same Element are very strong together, the four Elements interact by slowing down and limiting each other's effects, by stimulating and increasing the effects of the other, or by working together to produce a cooperative result.

Key Four: Interaction of Elements

1) SLOWING DOWN EFFECTS

WANDS (Fire) and CUPS (Water)
SWORDS (Air) and PENTACLES (Earth)

2) INTENSIFYING EFFECTS

WANDS (Fire) and SWORDS (Air)
CUPS (Water) and PENTACLES (Earth)

3) WORKING TOGETHER

WANDS (Fire) and PENTACLES (Earth)
CUPS (Water) and SWORDS (Air)

When these principles of Slowing Down, Intensifying and Working Together are firmly committed to memory, the following seemingly complicated, general relationships will be self-evident:

**THE ZODIAC TRUMPS AND
THEIR ELEMENTS**

FIRE CARDS = *Emperor, Strength, Temperance*
WATER CARDS = *Hanged Man, Death, Judgment*
AIR CARDS = *Justice, Star, Lover*
EARTH CARDS = *Devil, Hierophant, Hermit*

THESE CARDS SLOW DOWN
EACH OTHER'S ACTIONS

MAGICIAN (Uranus, Airy)—EMPRESS (Venus, Earthy)
WORLD (Saturn, Earthy)—MAGICIAN (Uranus, Airy)
HIGH PRIESTESS (Neptune, Watery)—TOWER (Mars, Fiery)
SUN (Sun, Fiery)—HIGH PRIESTESS (Neptune, Watery)
EMPRESS (Venus, Earthy)—CHARIOT (Mercury, Airy)
CHARIOT (Mercury, Airy)—WORLD (Saturn, Earthy)
WHEEL OF FORTUNE (Jupiter, Watery)—TOWER (Mars, Fiery)
SUN (Sun, Fiery)—WHEEL OF FORTUNE (Jupiter, Watery)
MOON (Moon, Watery)—SUN (Sun, Fiery)
TOWER (Mars, Fiery)—MOON (Moon, Watery)

THESE CARDS INTENSIFY
EACH OTHER'S ACTIONS

MAGICIAN (Uranus, Airy)—TOWER (Mars, Fiery)
HIGH PRIESTESS (Neptune, Watery)—WORLD (Saturn, Earthy)
EMPRESS (Venus, Earthy)—HIGH PRIESTESS (Neptune, Watery)
CHARIOT (Mercury, Airy)—TOWER (Mars, Fiery)
WHEEL OF FORTUNE (Jupiter, Watery)—EMPRESS (Venus, Earthy)
MOON (Moon, Watery)—EMPRESS (Venus, Earthy)
SUN (Sun, Fiery)—MAGICIAN (Uranus, Airy)
CHARIOT (Mercury, Airy)—SUN (Sun, Fiery)
WHEEL OF FORTUNE (Jupiter, Watery)—WORLD (Saturn, Earthy)
MOON (Moon, Watery)—WORLD (Saturn, Earthy)

THESE CARDS WORK
TOGETHER IN HARMONY

MAGICIAN (Uranus, Airy)—WHEEL OF FORTUNE
    (Jupiter, Watery)
HIGH PRIESTESS (Neptune, Watery)—MAGICIAN
    (Uranus, Airy)
EMPRESS (Venus, Earthy)—TOWER (Mars, Fiery)
CHARIOT (Mercury, Airy)—HIGH PRIESTESS (Neptune,
    Watery)
WHEEL OF FORTUNE (Jupiter, Watery)—CHARIOT
    (Mercury, Airy)
TOWER (Mars, Fiery)—WORLD (Saturn, Earthy)
MOON (Moon, Watery)—MAGICIAN (Uranus, Airy)
CHARIOT (Mercury, Airy)—MOON (Moon, Watery)
SUN (Sun, Fiery)—EMPRESS (Venus, Earthy)
WORLD (Saturn, Earthy)—SUN (Sun, Fiery)

For purposes of card interpretation the Trump Card of the
Zodiac which is the Cardinal Element is taken to represent the
whole Elemental suit. So:

> *The Emperor*, Aries, Fire, powers all Wands;
> *The Hanged Man*, Cancer, Water, powers all Cups;
> *Justice*, Libra, Air, powers all Swords; and
> *The Devil*, Capricorn, Earth, powers all Pentacles.

The word "rulership" is not used here. It is not said, for example,
that *The Emperor* rules all Wands. Signs do not rule. What these
Cardinal signs do is to define their element. So it is understood
that when *The Emperor* appears in a spread, he has a special

12

relationship to any Wands on the board. In his presence the operation of the Wands may become stronger and more certain. Their activity is definitely more obvious, as if *The Emperor* is shining a light to call attention to them. The same principle, of course, applies for the respective elements of *The Hanged Man*, *Justice*, and *The Hierophant*.

The Human Body and the Tarot

Definition of specific medical problems through the tarot, as with an astrological chart, depends very much upon the totality of cards on the board and is among the most difficult and advanced aspect of tarot reading, just as it is in astrology.

Traditionally parts of the body are assigned to Signs of the Zodiac. Illnesses however, are deemed to be specific to the planetary influence. As a general rule, one should start with the fact that *The Sun* rules the entire body, in its vitality, and *The Moon* is co-ruler of the body's functions. A very experienced reader must determine if the position of the Sun or Moon cards (especially if they appear together in a spread) is pointing toward an illness in a part of the body. Moreover, the relationship between the Zodiac Trumps and the Planetary Trumps may be extremely subtle and may require a considerable number of additional cards to create a clear picture.

PARTS OF THE BODY RELATED
TO THE ZODIAC TRUMPS

EMPEROR (Aries, ruled by Mars)
          Head, Skull, Face, Sight
LOVER (Gemini, ruled by Mercury)
          Arms, Shoulders, Hands, Lungs
STRENGTH (Leo, ruled by the Sun)
          Heart and Back, Spine, Right Eye of
          Male, Left Eye of Female
JUSTICE (Libra, ruled by Venus)
          Loins and Kidneys, Bladder
TEMPERANCE (Sagittarius, ruled by Jupiter)
          Liver, Thighs, Circulatory System
STAR (Aquarius, ruled by Uranus)
          Legs and Ankles
HIEROPHANT (Taurus, ruled by Venus)
          Throat and Neck, Vocal Chords
HANGED MAN (Cancer, ruled by The Moon)
          Breasts and Stomach, Digestion, Left Eye
          of Male, Right Eye of Female
HERMIT (Virgo, ruled by Mercury)
          Abdomen, Bowels
DEATH (Scorpio, ruled by Pluto)
          Sex Organs
DEVIL (Capricorn, ruled by Saturn)
          Knees, Skin, Bones, Spleen, Teeth,
          Hearing
JUDGMENT (Pisces, ruled by Neptune)
          Feet, Blood, Body Fluids

ILLNESSES RELATED TO
THE PLANETARY CARDS

FOOL (Pluto): Suicide, AIDS, problems related to radiation.

MAGICIAN (Uranus, the Higher Mercury): Fractures, lesions, spasmodic illnesses, disorders of the brain and nervous system, strokes.

HIGH PRIESTESS (Neptune): Anorexia, paranoia, hallucinations, anemias, drug addiction.

EMPRESS (Venus): Poisoning, hemorrhoids, blood poisoning.

CHARIOT (Mercury): Speech disorders, difficulties in breathing, nervous disorders, disabilities related to stress and excitement.

WHEEL OF FORTUNE (Jupiter): Diabetes, liver disease, pancreatitis.

TOWER (Mars): Fever, inflammations, surgeries, diseases of the eyes.

MOON (Moon): Physiochemical imbalances, allergies, eyesight defects, female sexual problems.

SUN (Sun): Heart disease, problems related to the upper spine, fainting spells, diseases that destroy tissues.

INITIAL QUESTIONS IN
A DIVINATION

First of all, it should be understood that this system can be learned slowly and there is nothing wrong with looking up attributions of the cards, after they have been encountered at least once. The theory is that even if meanings are not consciously recalled, nothing is lost to the unconscious which will more or less automatically influence the placement of the cards. In the beginning it may be necessary to refer frequently to this book in answering questions such as those suggested here.

15

How Many Cards of Each Element?

One can often define the nature of the question using four key categories determined by preponderance of an Element (both Minor Card and Trump Elements considered). This can help to determine how the cards are to be interpreted. The areas are: *Fire=Spiritual* (birth and death, creation, power, God); *Water=Mental* (love, friendship, art, music, hopes and dreams); *Air=Thought* (ideas, writing, languages, communication); and *Earth=Physical* (body and health, money and security). *The Magician* could mean great adventure in a Fire-dominated reading or it might mean a broken arm in an Earth-dominated reading if this idea is supported by other cards in the spread.

Where Do the Elements Fall?

If, for example, *The Emperor*, the primary card of Fire-Wands, appears in the upper left area of "thoughts and feelings," it may be reasonable to assume that desire is responsible for Fire activity in another part of the reading, even if it is in a Karmic area at the bottom right, meaning something beyond the person's control. It is extremely important to understand how the different parts of the divination, meaning all five sections on the board, relate to one another. Cards show interactions, especially those of the same suit or Element. And it is essential to appreciate which card causes something in another part of the reading, and from what point it is acting.

What is the "Aspect" of Each Trump?

Is a very mean card, like *The Ten of Cups*, next to *The Wheel of Fortune?* Is a neighboring card sufficient to actually influence one of the best cards in the deck in a negative way? Are there good cards next to *The Fool*, indicating positive influence of a group, or is *The Fool* next to *Death*, suggesting possible suicide? Does a card of success next to *The Tower* mean tremendous energy applied positively and aggressively, rather than the more usual interpretation of some accident or dreadful sudden event? The point is that there is a considerable range of possible meanings to each of the Keys, and one must immediately determine whether the card has something good or bad to say about the question by considering the cards beside it.

Specificity in Readings

If there is a general criticism of all forms of divination it is what might be called "the fortune cookie syndrome." Those who are scientifically minded have no qualms about pointing out the extent to which many readings are so general that they could apply to almost anyone. So credibility, to a lot of people, will depend upon conveying very specific information which turns out to be correct. Seeking a high statistical "predictive validity" may sound threatening although, in this regard, some may be consoled by the fact that fifty one percent is greater than chance.

Specifics come from experience. Understanding when *The Tower* refers to active sports and when it refers to a dreadful accident eventually develops. But no matter how experienced or inexperienced the reader may be, the common dominator is a belief that tarot reading involves something psychic that cannot be measured empirically.

The bottom line is a reader's fearless willingness to blurt out something ridiculous, stupid, and absolutely wrong! There is a mechanism here which some have described as "getting the personality out of the way," and allowing an "other" to come through.

THE FOOL

Pluto
(Kether, One)
The Aces
Rules: *Death* (Scorpio)

This is the root of all Elements and is the most powerful card of the deck. The whole tarot deck is potential in this card. Thus it interacts comfortably with all planetary cards. *The Fool* is identified with original thought or creative impulse which can mean the urge toward something new, or it can mean something that is hidden and, most of all, collective. In Jungian interpretation *The Fool* is never mindless or silly as it is sometimes interpreted in other systems. Most of all this card shows a group process of reproduction and regeneration— something radically new that affects more than the individual. Pluto, which refers to the masses and organized groups, rules Scorpio, thus *The Fool* rules *Death*. It has to do with reproduction and regeneration on a grand scale and, like Uranus and Neptune, its presence shows unimaginable power. ***General Meanings:*** The masses, collectivity, regeneration, rebirth, radical change, reproduction, rights administered for the good of all, the underworld, hidden things, specialization, lure of the public, crime, confinement, the dead, detectives, spy agencies, personal focus within the masses, psychoanalysis, resurrection, synthetics, plastics, atomic fission, sex drive, ideas ahead of their time, ideas which will not bear fruit until the next generation, a sociological urge, a situation where an organized group cuts out parasites to reorganize on more altruistic lines, foundations for advancement of human welfare, trade unions, potential for righteous indignation on behalf of society (not personal vindictiveness). ***Negative:*** mass-murder, suicide, AIDS, diseases related to radiation.

THE MAGICIAN

Uranus
(Chokmah, Two)
The Twos
The Kings
Rules: *The Star* (Aquarius)

Uranus, a higher octave of Mercury, rules Aquarius, thus *The Magician* rules *The Star*. Whenever this card appears in a spread it signifies the operation of something quite overwhelming. Almost no surrounding cards, no matter how ordinary, could mitigate the profound effects of *The Magician*. Uranus spurs brilliance and overpowering change which cannot be stopped. It breaks utterly with the past and is anarchistic, even fanatical. It is also completely spontaneous and may bring adventure of the most extraordinary sort. It is the essence of invention and innovation as brought about by the power of the will. *The Magician* can mean genius, invention, or a separation out of something unique. It signifies unique independence, totally uncontrolled activity, and a high degree of adventurous spontaneity. ***General Meanings:*** invention, innovation, suddenness, unusualness, adventure, separation or divorce, genius, homosexuality (note: this is a meaning of both Uranus and Mercury and is an assured interpretation in the presence of both *Magician* and *Chariot*), spontaneity, modernity, intuitive intellect, electronics, air travel, communications, research, science and invention, machinery, antiques, prophecy, mixed forms, broken lines, iconoclasm, aloofness, interdependence at any price, impulsiveness, rejection of authority and control. ***Negative:*** fanaticism, sarcasm, anarchy, fractures, ruptures, lesions, spasmodic disorders, diseases of the brain and nervous system, strokes.

19

THE HIGH PRIESTESS

Neptune
(Binah,Three)
The Threes
The Queens
Rules: *Judgment*
(Pisces)

Neptune rules Pisces, thus *The High Priestess* rules *Judgment*. Neptune has to do with social unrest, mobs, and the common people. It inspires mysticism and dreaming as well as illusion and deception. This is a card of psychic flow, of dreams, and of a love of mystery which may mean deception and falsehood. It is the essence of a mystic flow that affects social unrest, the behavior of deluded crowds, and the common man. It may also mean theatricality and music. The most important question that should be asked when this card appears in a spread is at what level it is functioning, and does it suggest falsehood or does it point toward a truly spiritual flow and connection to a rather restless group consciousness? *General Meanings:* Fantasy, the spiritual, delusion, everything false, all substitutes (fakes), mediumism, dreams, water, schemes, substitution, the psyche, gases, drugs, chemicals, anesthesia, theatricality, films, music, mobs, the common people, telepathy, psychic or occult faculties, martyrs, false promises, poisons, liquids, habit-forming drugs, love of mystery, eroticism, democratic and popular movements, prophets, spiritual counselors, philosophers, artistic and literary genius, martyrdom, masochism, eccentric behavior. *Negative:* lies, deception, anorexia, paranoia, hallucinations, anemia, glandular imbalance, drug addiction. The card can indicate self-deception or it can suggest that a person is being deceived by others.

20

THE EMPRESS

Venus
(Netzach, Seven)
The Sevens
Rules: *The Hierophant*
(Taurus) and
Justice (Libra)

Venus rules both Taurus and Libra, thus *The Empress* rules *The Hierophant* and *Justice*. A planet of romance and of beauty, Venus brings love and luxury and all that is artistic. *The Empress* means fruitfulness, expansiveness, and anything which indicates fertility, growth, luxuriance, and ornamentation. She refers to comfort, luxury, and the arts, as well as to romance and sociability. This is a card of ultimate maternal activities, of the mature woman who takes great pleasure in her family and who creates a secure and loving home. She is the natural source of the human condition and as the mother archetype there is a great deal more warmth in this card than in the first female of the deck, *The High Priestess*. This card almost always shows something pleasant and positive, and some aspect of real growth. But the blessings of *The Empress* can be taken to an extreme and a person may become slovenly and self-indulgent. ***General Meanings:*** aesthetics, femininity, beauty, ease, the arts, sociability, possessions, romance, marriage, luxuries, rewards, cash, jewelry and ornaments, sweets, women's clothing, fabrics, polished reflecting surfaces, good taste, affection and graciousness but somewhat patronizing, extremes of feeling. ***Negative:*** self-pity, self-indulgence, vanity, slothfulness, poisoning, diseases of the blood, infections, pustural diseases such as measles, kidney disease, venereal disease.

21

THE EMPEROR

Aries
Cardinal Fire
(All Wands)
Ruled by: *The Tower*
(Mars)

The ram is an outgoing and impulsive energy which makes its own rules. Thus the Arian *Emperor* is an assertive ruler whose leadership is powerful and well-considered. He directs the raw force of *The Tower*, Mars. A powerful energy which is potentially offensive and destructive is administered. *The Emperor* can mean a pioneering strength and vastly creative masculine energy applied, or it can mean the forceful application of reason and intelligence. Here is the general who assesses his situation and then acts decisively. He is also, of course, the primary father of the deck, the archetype which is the essence of the paternal role. It is the balance of father and mother which truly creates the family. She is the fruitful source, and he is the provider and protector. ***General Meanings:*** enterprise, powerful leadership, "rule or ruin." A person who dislikes authority, who does not take orders, who makes his own rules, and who insists on directing. The impulse here is more mental than emotional. This is a power of masculinity, of the military, of generals, of war and of war-makers. *The Emperor* is the avenger, the protector of a family. It is pure force under willful control that may be taken in any direction, aggression, impulsiveness, demanding, controlling, firm but fair. ***The Body:*** Head, skull, face, sight. ***Negative:*** arrogance, cruelty, dictatorial demands, anger and hostility. Under truly bad conditions, *The Emperor* can be a terrible card, one suggesting the worst abuses of which a father or other leader can be guilty.

THE HIEROPHANT

Taurus
Fixed Earth
Ruled by: *The Empress*
(Venus)

The Hierophant is temporal power, which may mean a government, a religious organization or some other organization to which the individual in question is subject. The relationship of the person to this government, church, or power group, is shown by the other cards. It can provide support, or it can be oppressive and adversarial to the individual. In any event, Taurus, the Bull, means an earthly control that is inherently determined, practical, and dutiful. It is slow and plodding, but a dangerous force when angered. It is the "will to form," the dream-thought of a material kingdom proposed by its ruler, *The Empress. The Hierophant* is practical and determined and is very thorough in all that it does. It is very plodding and certain and will persist in its course in spite of any obstacles. The card often demonstrates the will and determination of the person in question while surrounding cards indicate whether the endeavor will be successful. ***General Meanings:*** As Taurus the card shows determination, clinging to ideas once accepted, ready acknowledgement of mistakes. Love of justice and truth, plodding activities, fear of offending, love of comfort, dislike of pain, dislike of argument, creating a beautiful home, determination, practicality, thoroughness, attention to duty. ***The Body:*** Throat and neck, vocal chords. ***Negative:*** overeating, a taste for the garish and gaudy, unreasonableness. Under negative aspects *The Hierophant* can show an almost destructive stubbornness, a complete unwillingness to move from an unreasonable position.

THE LOVER

Gemini
Mutable Air
Ruled by: *The Chariot*
(Mercury)

T*he Lover* is a union of opposites and an ability to discriminate between things which appear to be very different. Gemini, The Twins, are equal and opposing energies which may show two sides of a question or which may pull in two different directions. *The Lover* personifies the mercurial tendencies of its ruler, *The Chariot*, to swiftly change course or to (enigmatically) move in two directions at once. The card may also mean frustration and indecision about two alternatives. The key here is adaptability and an intellectual inquiry. When *The Lover* appears it shows great intellectual abilities, skill at writing, taking great pleasure in novelties although being easily bored. But since this is a Trump card, a "Key," these qualities are not necessarily those of an individual, but can also be qualities of a group or of a given situation. The card could be central in a decision of some sort, perhaps legal, which is indicated by surrounding cards. At its most positive this means the ability to see both sides of a question. The card may refer to a situation in which there is no clear resolution or which could evolve in different ways. *General Meanings:* adaptability, thinking, mental abilities, discrimination, curiosity and inquiry, seeing both sides of a question, good memory, learning, hatred of the dull and plodding, impulsiveness, cleverness, sensitivity and tendency to be high strung. *The Body:* arms, shoulders, hands, lungs. *Negative:* unpredictability, uncertainty, inability to choose, rash judgments.

THE CHARIOT

Mercury
(Hod, Eight)
The Eights
Rules: *The Lover* (Gemini)
The Hermit (Virgo)

Mercury rules both Virgo and Gemini, thus *The Chariot* rules *The Hermit* and *The Lover*. Mercury is the planet of communications, of intelligence, of language, and of the law. A most important aspect of Mercury is its neutrality; it is the vehicle by which ideas are transmitted. It shows the delivery of news, of letters, and of communications of any sort, including contracts, thus specific interpretations depend on neighboring cards. *The Chariot* represents all written materials, ranging from creative novels and poems to accomplished works of scholarship. It is, at best, the transmission of thoughts and ideas and can also refer to short travels. ***General Meanings:*** speech, memory, intelligence, neutrality, alertness, understanding, diversity, communication, activity, travel, close relatives, writing, humor, expression of opinions, strong mental abilities, accounts, details, vehicles, contracts, papers connected with money, legal documents, writing materials, anything connected with education, the will to action, perception of weight, size, order, color, etc., pure reason, diet. ***Negative:*** anxiety, indecision, excitability, nervousness, cunning, craftiness, subtlety, gossip, wittiness, apparent brilliance but not really profound, a technician whose proficiency is superficial, one who is has some literary skills but is not the best writer, behavioral disorders, nervous disorders, disability from excitement, stress, headaches, loss of memory, digestive problems.

STRENGTH

Leo
Fixed Fire
Ruled By: *The Sun*
(The Sun)

The tarot card of *Strength* is one not only of strength, but also of creative energy. The Lion of Leo is at once regal and powerful. Its animal strength is held in check by intelligence and by a strong sense of inner peace. *Strength* embodies all of the qualities of its ruler, *The Sun*, the light of which may inspire, but the extreme heat of which may destroy. This is a card which channels solar energy and which represents great power and enthusiasm. It is at once commanding and magnanimous. A person may be very quick to anger, but there is no holding of grudges. When the card of *Strength* appears in a spread it may represent qualities of an individual, either the person in question or someone close, which are applied to a specific situation. For example, if a problem is indicated, the card may suggest that the response is intelligent and effective. Under some circumstances the card can refer to the activity of a group which relates to the individual. ***General Meanings:*** a channel for solar energy, paternal strength ("at one with the Father"), administration, magnanimity, dislike of pettiness, exercise of power from behind (dislike of prominence, but desire to rule), quick to anger, but not holding grudges, enthusiastic. ***The Body:*** Heart, and back, spine, right eye of male, left eye of female. ***Negative:*** There may be a streak of feline cruelty. Other negative possibilities include loud clothes or behaviors which can call attention to oneself, including making scenes in public places. At worst the card can signal falsehood, meanness, and deceit.

THE HERMIT

T*he Hermit* is the Light Bearer who brings inspiration and guidance, sometimes from above and sometimes from a more mundane source. Virgo is a very orderly and controlled sign of Earth. Under positive aspects it is honest and thoughtful, having high ideals which are usually "grounded." This card, like *The Lover*, is ruled by *The Chariot*. *The Hermit* expresses all of the brilliant intellectual qualities of Mercury which are here "grounded." Thoughtfulness, industriousness, and honesty are the keynote. And although there may be high ideals, a person maintains a rational overview. In fact reason over force is the keynote here. *The Hermit* may also be understood as the benevolent guide, a teacher who is, at a very high spiritual level, an initiator. So, to some extent, whatever results from the activities of this card can be considered to be an important part of life's learning experiences. Of course, the experiences necessary for growth may not always be pleasant. ***General Meanings:*** Guidance, honesty, revealing, light-bearing, thoughtfulness, contemplation, industriousness, high ideals, but always grounded, quick temper, but not combative, preferring reason to force, withdrawal, ingeniousness, discrimination, active, and mercurial. ***The Body:*** Abdomen, bowels. ***Negative:*** pettiness, holding grudges and other reversals of the general meanings indicated. Because this is such an inherently positive card, the forces required to make it negative must be substantial.

27

WHEEL OF FORTUNE

Jupiter
(Chesed, Four)
The Fours
Rules: *The Lover* (Gemini)

Jupiter rules Sagittarius, thus *The Wheel of Fortune* rules *Temperance.* Jupiter means good fortune, expansiveness, harmony, and success. The presence of this planet is almost always a positive sign. *The Wheel of Fortune* means destiny, or fate, and often a bonanza. This is a card of hope, of enthusiasm, and of successful opportunity. It is optimistic, showing generosity and extravagance. It may represent the coming of wealth, but it may also suggest an overabundance of wealth which borders on gluttony. For the most part this is a card of good fortune, although under the most dire of conditions it may point to the coming of an unavoidable bad situation. But even in this, it is likely that the negative aspects are necessary to bring about something better. *The Wheel of Fortune* may also neutralize the bad effect of another card, creating a sort of "standoff." In a reading this card should not, in any case, be viewed simplistically as "things going well." In concert with the surrounding cards, a great deal of information can be conveyed about how good fortune is handled. It can sometimes be wasted. ***General Meanings:*** Very broad meanings include expansiveness, enthusiasm, good fortune, opportunity, extravagance, people associated with religion, benevolence, mercy, knowledge, wealth, success, judgment in one's favor, commerce, inheritance, education, hope, idealism, creative faculties, health, harmony, law as harmony, love of beauty, optimism, order, education, social gatherings, theatres, industrialists, capitalists, the judiciary, ecclesiastical leaders.

JUSTICE

Libra
Cardinal Air
(All Swords)
Ruled by: *The Empress*
(Venus)

The balanced scales show the perfect cooperation of persons, of ideas, or of situations. The fact that *The Empress* rules *Justice* shows that justice is only possible within the confines of her world because true justice is a human concept. Taken at its most simplistic, the card means justice, equilibrium, and fairness as well as balance and poise. And although *Justice* is the essence of cooperation, there is little tolerance for questioning a decision that has been made. The order of justice is precise and final. This is also a card of mediation and of general balance in all situations; there are no extremes here. To some extent this can be a card of control in life. It can mean weighing all of the possibilities and coming to a conclusion about direction. It can also mean the end of uncertainty and anxiety as a decision is reached. Time framework is of particular significance in this card; *Justice* may mean a continuing process whereby balance is maintained, in which case it represents a sequence of regular decisions, or it may refer to a specific past or present condition. This card should be compared to *Judgment*, which is more specific. ***General Meanings:*** balance, poise, the arts, music, writing, justice, neatness, and precision. This may show a person who hates messy, dirty, work, and who is touchy about having motives questioned, no matter how distorted ideas of justice may be. Whatever the circumstances, one is courteous, pleasant and agreeable, though often moody—with emotional highs and lows. ***The Body:*** Loins and kidneys, bladder. ***Negative***: outbursts of great anger, irrational demands.

THE HANGED MAN

Cancer
Cardinal Water
(All Cups)
Ruled by:
The Moon (Moon)

A radical change of perspective; a completely different point of view. The Crab, a powerful sign of water, shows a connection to something universal, a love of home, and an underlying psychic flow which is logically directed by its ruler, *The Moon*. *The Hanged Man* is attached to an "other," which may be universal or may be the home. There is tremendous sensitivity here, which may be highly psychic and mediumistic. This is, in many respects, a very odd card because it can point to a situation which is quite different than it appears to be on the surface. The figure floats in the water of consciousness which is a philosophical reversal of the material condition. It is the total opposite of Capricorn/ Earth. Thus the love of "home" may mean love of the ultimate spiritual home, or the reference may be to the earthly (family) home. What should be understood here is that although the general meanings given for this card are quite basic, this card can represent far more than the sum of its apparent parts.

General Meanings: reversal, a completely opposite point of view, psychic activity, connection to the universal, love of home, strong sense of family, mediumism, fondness for change and changing conditions, sensitivity, feeling of responsibility for children, roaming the world in the course of business but gladly returning home, vigorous defense of what is believed to be right, imaginative, economical, persistent. ***The Body:*** Breasts and stomach, digestion, left eye of male, right eye of female. ***Negative:*** confusion, lack of focus.

DEATH

This card shows transition, healing, sometimes death, and sometimes even birth. This is Scorpio, the serpent force of sex. The Scorpion can be exciting, fiery and dangerous or it can be regenerative, magical, and magnetic. That *Death* is ruled by *The Fool* means that it expresses the relationship of the individual in transition (either changing completing or actually dying) to the Plutonian collective. Sexuality is the most common meaning to be derived here, depending upon the bordering cards. *Death* is always magnetic and mystical. In Jungian terms, to experience the transition shown in the card as crossing a bridge on which there can be no return, is return to the Cosmic Mother who is the source of generation and, thus, of regeneration. It is the serpent power of this card which carries a person from one place of consciousness to another. And here a point about the fluidity of *Death* should be considered: The card's ruler, *The Fool*, is everything. Each of the cards is *The Fool* in one guise or another, male and female alike. And *The Fool* has the capacity to move effortlessly from one condition to another. Thus *Death* is a card which calls into question the very nature of time and of space, particularly insofar as its transitions are only apparent. ***General Meanings:*** generation, serpent force, mystical flow, magnetic current, resourcefulness, sarcasm when angered, trustworthiness with secrets, vivid imagination, inner power, executive ability, constructive power, readinesss to fight, a tireless worker. ***The Body:*** Sex organs. ***Negative:*** hostility, violence, irrationality.

31

TEMPERANCE

Sagittarius
Mutable Fire
Ruled by:
The Wheel of Fortune
(Jupiter)

Here two or more different forces are combined, resulting in a balance of opposites and harmony. This a process, rather than a simple event and usually involves trial and experimentation, testing and verification—much like an alchemical process where elements are combined to produce something new. Bringing the forces of *Temperance* to bear means an ability to distinguish outer (apparent) motives from the inner truth about why something is happening. And in this there is a very certain goal. Sagittarius, The Archer, has a definite aim and a clear target. So this can be called a card of searching and of intention. A person starts the process of combining forces with a specific goal. *Temperance* shows aspiration, zeal, trial and experimentation. Outer appearance is separated from inner reality. The rulership of *The Wheel of Fortune* shows the card's innate expansiveness, generosity, and love of frankness. ***General Meanings:*** testing, trial and experimentation, verification, tentativeness, separation, distinguishing between outer appearance and inner motive power, definiteness of aim resulting from zeal of aspiration, philosophical overview, charity and generosity, interest easily aroused, dislike of peoples' suffering, frank and open, hatred of double-dealing and concealment. The most mundane expression of this card is a love of sports and of hunting, friendliness, frankness, sympathetic, conservative and thoughtful. ***The Body:*** Liver, thighs, circulatory system. ***Negative:*** Aspiration becomes thoughtless, driving ambition.

THE DEVIL

Capricorn
Cardinal Earth
(All Pentacles)
Ruled by: *The World*
(Saturn)

The Devil, which is Cardinal Earth and the Sign of Capricorn, should not be considered to be a fundamentally evil card. It is, rather, a steadfast and immovable material force, and sometimes one of animal sensuality (recalling that Pan was half-goat). It shows control in the condition of matter and is thoughtful, serious, and often ambitious. Capricorn, The Goat, is strong and secure on the mountain where it lives representing, as it does, the base point of matter. It is, of course, ruled by *The World* which means the earthly condition. *The Devil* may be an employer who is cautious and frugal. It may positively represent the abilities of an executive, or it may negatively suggest the enslavement of material desires. It can also mean initiation and an introduction to the true cosmic order, for to understand the material condition is the first step in understanding the patterns of the universe, as is expressed in the axiom "as above, so below." In philosophical terms the Devil/Capricorn may be thought of as complete limitation. The life force is locked into place; a person perceives nothing beyond the rock solid perspective of matter. *General Meanings:* concreteness, intensive labor, changes brought about by time, extremes of height and depth, an employer, executive ability, conservative, persistent, cautious, frugal, serious, not easily discouraged, considers intuition and psychism to be nonsense. *The Body:* Knees, skin, bone, spleen, teeth, hearing. *Negative:* blind obedience, coldness, suspicion.

33

THE TOWER

In almost every system of tarot interpretation *The Tower* is considered to show a very unpleasant and sudden event, such as an automobile accident. Underlying here is Mars ruling Aries, which in tarot terms means that *The Tower* rules *The Emperor*. Mars is raw power applied. Its influence is generally called warring and destructive, but, like the making of war itself, there is always a specific reason that its energies are applied, although that reason may not be at all apparent. There are no accidents, and cards around and related to *The Tower* should give some idea of why the event has occurred. This can be a card of energy applied after thought. It may represent an action which is the result of a decision—a premeditated event, or it can show something beyond apparent control. Whatever happens, whether violence, quarreling, destruction, upheaval, or general danger, the result is a change which is always definitive. A completely new condition results, one which may be quite good. The fall from *The Tower* can essentially force a renewal. ***General Meanings:*** applied energy, accident, force, sex, danger, executiveness, mechanics, speed, upheaval, heat, anger, courage, weapons, enforcement, military, steel, cutlery, instruments of war, sports, enterprise, a strong and aggressive friend. ***Negative:*** violence, crimes of violence, criminals, thieves, antagonism, destruction, a vengeful enemy, revenge, fever, inflammation, surgery, epidemics of contagious diseases, eye problems.

THE STAR

Aquarius
Fixed Air
Ruled by:
The Magician (Uranus)

T*he Star* is a card of inspiration and knowledge which refers to meditation and to the most profound processes of thought. In a reading it can operate at two practical levels. First, it gives hope: whenever it occurs it shows that there is inner activity at work and that no matter how dismal a situation may be, there is hope and divine support. It can also mean that there is a hidden source of help which is going to show up. Second it can, by its position "show the way" and suggest a course of action. If, for example, *The Star* is related to a King or a Queen, it may be interpreted to mean that this is a man or a woman to whom one should turn for advice or help. The spiritual and mental activity of this card tells a great deal about the cards around it. *The Star* suggests each person's point of contact with universal powers beyond the individual personality. It is the appearance of each person's "Inner Star," a light of immeasurable brightness. In Jungian terms this is an aspect of Anima, the first female, which is essentially guided by Animus, the first male, shown in tarot by *The Magician*. So *The Star* is deeply linked into the original creative patterns of the Universe. ***General Meanings:*** Meditation, dawning of truth, thoughtfulness, friendliness, the scientist, the truth seeker, unselfish love, the humanitarian principle, kind and friendly, warm, cheerful, frank, open. ***The Body:*** Legs and ankles. ***Negative:*** repression of feelings, dependency upon others, complete and pathological withdrawal.

THE MOON

The Moon
(Yesod, Nine)
The Nines
Rules: *The Hanged
Man* (Cancer)

The moon rules Cancer, thus *The
Moon* rules *The Hanged Man*. The
moon is a murky "planet" which "waxes
and wanes." When this card appears in a spread it can point to
intentional or unintentional deception and to real dishonesty,
depending upon surrounding cards. It can warn of a dark and
even dangerous situation. This can be a card of great fear and
of insecurity, or it can be a card of beautiful romance because
it represents emotional flow and personal perception, a condition of dream images where rational thought has little bearing.
The position of the card in a reading may suggest the ebb and
flow of a matter, dark dreams, possibly a severe test. One way
or the other, whenever it appears, the reader should see it as
pointing to an illusory condition which may be an invention but
which certainly cannot be trusted. This is a card of visions and
of shifting moods which may be alcohol or drug induced. *The
Moon* can mean the home, the mother, or women in general. It
can mean childbirth. It can also mean travel or change. ***General
Meanings:*** dreams, nightmares, rhythm, imagination, mother,
maternal instincts, home, the house, soft, smooth substances,
focus of experience, moods, alcohol or drugs, fluids, digestion,
menstruation, peacefulness, faith, hope, and charity, travel by
water, all common employments, inferior positions, employ-
ment involving water, seamen, fishermen, romantic, kind,
visionary. ***Negative:*** emotional depression, mental instability,
laziness, endocrine imbalance, allergies, female disorders.

THE SUN

The Sun
(Tiphareth, Six)
The Sixes
The Princes
Rules: *Strength* (Leo)

The light and warmth of *The Sun* will enervate any situation and almost always indicates a positive influence on the matter in question. At its most positive, *The Sun* shows riches, glory, and an influx of everything that is pleasant. It is a card of great power and control as was personified in the great King Louis XIV who called himself "The Sun King." *The Sun* shows the most intense (male) life energy and growth, both spiritual and physical. The card, which may mean children, represents a source of warmth, vitality, and character illumination. Truth, generosity, faith, and honor are essential here. When the card appears in a spread it often involves the awakening of a new perspective and a new way of looking at life. ***General Meanings:*** Insofar as *The Sun* is the center of Life, it has a wide range of meanings including life itself, energy, health, vitality, maleness, energy, ego, Self, authority, illumination of character, magnanimity, money, royalty, influence, faith, honor, theatre, loyalty, children, reputation, generosity, truth, precious metals, diamonds, things valuable, fame, generation of vital force, individuality as ego consciousness, power, executive, heads of government, love of polite formalities and of ritual, generosity, truthfulness. ***The Body:*** heart, spine, right eye of male, left eye of female, circulation. ***Negative:*** ostentation, despotism, heart problems, problem of upper spine, fevers, breakdown of tissues, fainting spells, organic ailments, spleen diseases.

37

JUDGMENT

Judgment shows a condition of moody and isolated introspection in which forces behind appearance are revealed. Thus it also relates to spiritualism and to psychism. There is here a withdrawal from the world into a condition of self-criticism and self-evaluation (greatly affected by the rulership of *The High Priestess,* Neptune). This card is Pisces and the dual fish of the sign swim in the waters of the personal unconscious. The card shows a very strong elemental quality of activity within water which is also seen in *The Hanged Man* and when interpreting *Judgment* it should be kept in mind that the *High Priestess* is the crystalline clear water from which the murky waters of *Judgment* ultimately derive and to which there will ultimately be a return. *Judgment* can mean the outcast who is really The Messiah. It points to a romantic and imaginative person, one who is generally benevolent, kind, and generous and who enjoys good company. This is a person slow to anger, but who is capable of taking serious revenge—again suggesting that there is a great deal going on under the surface which is not seen. **General Meanings:** mysticism and psychism, forces behind appearance, inhibition of natural expression, self-denial, withdrawal, all comprehension, The Messiah, the outcast, a romantic and imaginative person who is generally benevolent and generous and enjoys good company. A person slow to anger, but who can take revenge. **The Body:** Feet. **Negative:** spiritual pride, isolation and moody introspection, tormented by fantasies.

THE WORLD

Saturn
(Malkuth, Ten)
The Tens
The Princesses
Rules: *The Devil*
(Capricorn)

S aturn is the great tester which, like the earthly condition itself may bring great sorrow. It is weighty and slow, defining in the course of its path through the heavens, the very meaning of time. It has to do with the earth, practical matters, restraints, frustration, delay, and perhaps sorrow. Time is most important to this card for the Saturnian influence is defining of the earthly life process and brings old age in its path. Sometimes there is selfishness and avarice; sometimes there is depression. This is a condition which is one-sided and myopic. *The World* shows structure and a conservative point of view which may be narrow-minded if not secretive and overly-cautious. In a tarot reading its appearance may suggest that a person is being somehow trapped or weighted down in a situation. ***General Meanings:*** structure, sorrow, land, agriculture, heavy materials, lead, old matters, old people, earth, slowness, deliberateness, concrete creative faculties, an ultra-conservative point of view, narrow-mindedness, isolation, civil servants, minor state executives, conservative business, dealing in land, laborers, builders, ambition, delay, wisdom, concentration, the Inner Father, elders, materialism, time, mines, restraints, insurance, caves, ruins, corpses, graves, secretive, cautious, prudent, patient. ***Negative:*** avarice, fears and morbid conditions, accidental falls, sorrow, envy, chronic illness, colds, arthritis and arteriosclerosis, Alzheimer's, diseases of old age.

WANDS
(FIRE, FAMILY OF THE EMPEROR)

Slowed down by Cups (Water)
Increased by Swords (Air)
Works with Pentacles (Earth)

KING OF WANDS
THE AGGRESSIVE FATHER
Roots: *Emperor*
Sun in Aries, Moon in Aries

This is a man who is forceful and independent, who says what he thinks, but who may be somewhat eccentric and demanding. He is essentially a sympathetic person who believes that he lives in a creative mental world unknown to others. Because *The King of Wands* has both sun and the moon in Aries, both inner and outer aspects of the man are totally fiery. The energies of *The Sun* expressed through *The Emperor* (Cardinal Fire) produce a man who is a dynamo of outgoing energy. His thoughts are highly independent, pioneering and self-reliant. He is assertive, and often impulsive. His world of inner feelings, *The Moon*, is full and dynamic, sparkling with creativity. A person with such a makeup will, by definition, feel that his very creativity and dynamism sets him apart from others who are incapable of sharing his thoughts and feelings. He is sympathetic and can be extremely kind and generous. But seeing things only from his own perspective tends to make him very selfish. In some situations this double Aries can be arrogant, demanding, and abrasive, caring nothing for what other people think.

QUEEN OF WANDS
THE STYLISH MOTHER
Roots: *Emperor, Hanged Man*
Sun in Aries, Moon in Cancer

The Queen of Wands is a woman who is intelligent, strong-willed, sensitive, and ambitious. She is stylish, subtle, and amusing, but is subject to swings of mood and can devastate someone who crosses her. She loves her home and fiercely protects her children from what she sees to be a hostile outside world. Her thoughts are outgoing and dynamic, but they are not so radical as the King, who is pure fire. Here the primarily fiery personality is mitigated by water; thoughts are refined by the balance of the purest feeling producing an individual who is very subtle, stylish, and amusing. The Queen is strong-willed, but that will is directed with sensitivity and a certain indescribable idealism. The roots of her feelings in the watery unconscious of *The Hanged Man* provide a special security and balance. Thus she is described as "dependent upon home" and "protective of her children." On the negative side, to be a fiery temperament drawn to water is not always easy. She is subject to swings of mood and can at one moment be incredibly charming and engaging and at the next moment be extremely vicious.

41

PRINCE OF WANDS
THE AFFECTIONATE SON
Roots: *Emperor, Justice*
Sun in Aries, Moon in Libra

This prince is caring and observant, a good judge of people and situations who tends to act rashly without thinking. He is a fine friend who enjoys parties and games and who loves to love, but who tends to be quite fickle. *The Prince of Wands* shares the passionate thoughts of his parents, the King and Queen, but he expresses them in ways which are charming and diplomatic. His feelings, rooted in *Justice*, are intense but they are very orderly. This is a young man who is cooperative, friendly, and who leans toward art and music. He is a quick thinker who is more practical than philosophical; he wants to do things. Because Aries and Libra are opposites on the Wheel of the Zodiac, *The Prince of Wands* is the perfect expression of Aries. Everything here is in balance. The openness of *The Prince of Wands* to the ideas and feelings of others tends to make him somewhat clairvoyant. So when this card appears, not as a specific person but representing qualities of a King or of a Queen, clairvoyance may be involved. It may also mean fame or at least some special prominence.

PRINCESS OF WANDS
THE CLEVER DAUGHTER
Roots: *Emperor, Devil*
Sun in Aries, Moon in Capricorn

Although she appears outgoing, this princess is actually insecure and vulnerable. She can be warm and loving, but can also be cruel and back-biting, reflecting her own frequent feelings of hostility and depression. *The Princess of Wands* brings a special perspective to practical matters. She is determined, positive and ambitious, an especially inquisitive person, wanting always to get to the bottom of things and to understand how things work. She is quick to figure out how others think. Her talents make her quite good in business and invariably land her in a position of leadership where she tends to domineer—an unconscious mechanism which makes her feel safe. She needs attention and praise because of the profound insecurities which lurk beneath her appearance of self-confidence. She must be certain that she is in control of her environment and of those around her. She also finds security in collecting material possessions and so loves to shop. At her worst she may be extraordinarily selfish, demanding, domineering, and a generally unpleasant and murky presence.

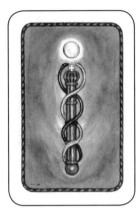

ACE OF WANDS
BIRTH AND DEATH
Roots: *Fool, Emperor*
Pluto in Aries

T he Root of Action, dynamic new beginnings, overwhelming and revolutionary change. This is either the advent of something new, or it is the end of something. It is, in any event, an overwhelming process, a total and complete change. This is the card of actual birth and death (the *Death* card is usually one of transition). The passionate, transforming energy, which may mean action and confrontation, is not for the faint of heart. It may mean a new profession. It may mean a new set of concepts about art, literature, government, or religion. It is raw power, unbridled for the individual or for society. It can mean the birth and death of nations, as seen, for example, in the French revolution. In a reading, the nature of this action will be shown by related cards. What happens can be either good or bad and, like anything completely new, what will ultimately come from this, like the child growing up, may not be at all certain.

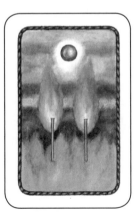

TWO OF WANDS
INVENTION
Roots: *Magician, Emperor*
Uranus in Aries

R ashness, creative inventiveness, an idea which is brilliant and original—product of a completely free and independent mind. In this card *The Magician*'s Uranian qualities of suddenness and invention are magnificently expressed through the Element of Fire. His independence and creative intellect cause something totally new and previously unthought of, to burst upon the scene. A work of such absolute genius is very much a part of the operation of *The Magician*. In this the single-mindedness of the inventor may be very irritating to others. And, in fact, the inventor generally has little support for his work in that no precedent exists.

THREE OF WANDS
FANTASY
Roots: *High Priestess, Emperor*
Neptune in Aries

Hidden currents of collective energy; a subtle yet powerful flow, like the undercurrent of a river. This Three shows initiation, mysticism, religion, and the occult as the deep and dark waters of Neptune meet the Martian fire of Aries. It is a card of hidden currents of controlling energy within the collective unconscious and it cannot be overstated that this is a collective energy; it is not individual. There is a loss of individuality to something greater. Imagination and fantasy flow. The deepest secrets of religion and of the occult are here. At a more mundane level this may mean an outpouring of benevolence and charity, or it may suggest travel for its own sake. Under the worst aspects, fantasies may be uncontrolled and lead to madness.

FOUR OF WANDS
SUCCESS
Roots: *Emperor, Wheel of Fortune*
Jupiter in Aries

Personal ability and driving ambition pay off. What happens is the result of personal ability and effort. The person is an innovator, a true pioneer. A plan is carefully laid and carried out with inspiration and enthusiasm. There is no change once one's mind is made up; an intelligent, self-assured person is almost pig-headed. As *The Four of Wands* is attached to *The Wheel of Fortune* and to *The Emperor*, the "success" of this card is self-evident. And since *The Emperor*/Aries stands first in the Zodiac, this card may signal the beginning of something wonderful. However, *The Four of Wands*' projects are never entirely without risk. The energy which must be expended may be too forceful, causing loss of money or profession as well as emotional and physical stress.

FIVE OF WANDS
ASSERTIVENESS
Roots: *Tower, Emperor*
Mars in Aries

Action for good or bad. Combativeness and originality. An attack which may be aggressive and impulsive is carried out without regard for outcome. Great personal courage may be involved—such as a person risking life for another, or a reputation may be put on the line for something in which one deeply believes. Since *The Tower*/Mars rules *The Emperor*/Aries this is an extremely powerful and dynamic card. There is an outgoing force, raw power which is applied to something, often without consideration for the effect because the Five of Wands is a card of raw action, not of thought. Of course, such impulsiveness and rashness may cause problems. The creative energy may be rapidly dissipated. Or the person may behave in a way which is thoughtless, even arbitrary and tyrannical.

SIX OF WANDS
STRONG LEADERSHIP
Roots: *Sun, Emperor*
Sun in Aries

This is the key leadership card of the tarot deck. It shows headstrong and impulsive behavior, love of challenge and of difficult situations. The person, who is self-assured and somewhat egocentric, is always ready for a fight or for a new adventure. The more competition the better. Difficult situations are handled with great skill. Dual fiery qualities of the Sun and of the Martian currents of Aries show the impulsiveness and volatility of a general eager to lead troops into battle and looking forward to the fray. Great loyalty is shown toward subordinates, who feel great affection toward their leader. It is unlikely that *The Six of Wand*s will ever appear in a losing situation, but the leader's actions are not necessarily for the good. It is possible that leadership may be bad. A person may be completely insensitive to the feelings of others and may lie and deceive subordinates. At worst, control may be exercised in violent and aggressive ways.

SEVEN OF WANDS
PASSION
Roots: *Empress, Emperor*
Venus in Aries

Infatuation burns out quickly. Hasty marriage. Money and love come fast and are wasted. This is a very volatile situation where the two figures are immediately attracted to each other, but their passion is quickly expended. The principle here is that there is nothing to stabilize a relationship between them; whatever experience this is must be fleeting. The card may mean attraction to another person or it may have to do with money, material objects or pleasurable things which are more or less wasted.

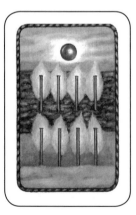

EIGHT OF WANDS
LITERARY ACTIVITY
Roots: *Chariot, Emperor*
Mercury in Aries

A work of true originality, even genius, which is rapidly produced. This could mean books, articles, or public speaking. In the kingdom of *The Emperor* the *The Charioteer* has unique abilities of language and communication and creates a remarkable literary work, rapidly and effortlessly. The emphasis here is on the dynamism of the process by which the work appears, as opposed to what happens in *The Eight of Swords*. *The Charioteer*, a Shakespeare or a Tolstoy, produces in an unstoppable burst of genius.

NINE OF WANDS
ANGER AND VOLATILITY
Roots: *Moon, Emperor*
Moon in Aries

Raw emotions and irrational impulses may suddenly explode, then just as suddenly dissipate. The card may show mental instability. It is rooted in the Moon's intense emotion, in dark shadows, in nightmares, and in the deepest fears and terrors. Emotional disturbance may be manifested as a generalized hostility toward co-workers and family. There may be threats and secret plots. Scandal may suddenly explode. Unresolved inner tensions may surface without warning. When this card appears in the upper left of a reading, the area of hidden thoughts and feelings, it may be a warning that beneath a calm surface a person may be mentally ill, perhaps psychotic, and perhaps even a serious threat. The energies of this card are, by definition, hostile and dangerous.

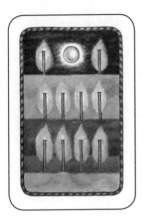

TEN OF WANDS
CONTROL OVER OTHERS
Roots: *World, Emperor*
Saturn in Aries

The *Ten of Wands* shows the pinnacle of authority and careful management of a structured group. It represents, for example, management success in a large company. Under good aspects, there is a well-conceived plan of control, a well-reasoned use of executive power. If the card is badly aspected, the person at the top may feel isolated and lonely. Under bad aspects the management plan may be badly organized, and there may be defensiveness and irritability.

CUPS
(WATER, FAMILY OF THE HANGED MAN)

Slowed down by Wands (Fire)
Increased by Pentacles (Earth)
Works with Swords (Air)

KING OF CUPS
THE INTELLECTUAL FATHER
Roots: Hanged Man, Emperor
Sun in Cancer, Moon in Aries

Possessing an agile, creative, mind, this King lives in an isolated world of thought. A sensitive daydreamer, he may withdraw into fantasies and shows little of himself to others. His actions are expressive of his deep roots in the unconscious mind. He is very insular, very wrapped up in his own mental experiences, and is generally isolated from most others who cannot share his dream world. Being capable of great creative intellectual activity and of considerable leadership, he is extremely independent and perceives that he brings to any situation a unique and understanding overview. His thoughts and world of imagination are dynamically expressed; he is unhappy being inactive for a long period of time. His mind is too active to rest in any set place for very long. An innate rebelliousness and tendency to do things impulsively may bring tremendous problems to himself and to others. So *The King of Cups* is a person whose ideas are rapidly expressed or acted upon with little or no concern for any consequences. Whenever this card appears one should look to the possibility that a plan may have been rashly imposed.

QUEEN OF CUPS
THE EMOTIONAL MOTHER
Roots: *Hanged Man*
Sun in Cancer, Moon in Cancer

Here is a sensitive and affectionate person. She is loyal, charming, entertaining, and of strong moral character, disliking those who break rules. Her sense of order keeps her emotional personality under control. This Queen is pure Water and is a contrast to *The King of Wands* who is pure Fire. The term "emotional" as used here is accurate but hardly begins to suggest the qualities of this figure. She represents, in Jungian terms, the collective unconscious functioning through the personal unconscious: hers are the attributes of the collective mind expressed through the individual mind. Obviously, therefore, she has two primary characteristics. The first is imagination that is almost unbounded. The second is a sense of order that can be called "old structure," a framework for things that is powerful and by which everything is measured. The collective unconscious imposes "rules" which are culturally-determined. But *The Queen of Cups* is also changeable. Imagination is, by definition, fluid, and life can become the stuff of which dreams are made. Out of control, or badly aspected, this Queen might become totally irrational, if not insane.

PRINCE OF CUPS
THE CHARMING SON
Roots: *Hanged Man, Justice*
Sun in Cancer, Moon in Libra

The Prince of Cups is a sparkling and romantic young man who is self-centered and superficial and who is constantly being pursued by people who find him attractive. But he is not one to ever settle down. He is capricious and elusive, loves to play around, and despite his attempt to avoid conflict, and his fear of being hurt, may unintentionally cause friction. The creative abilities of *The Prince of Cups* are harmonious, although his nature is essentially emotional and fanciful. He is a delightful person who is drawn to art, to music, and to pleasures of all sorts. He is a playful friend, but he lacks discipline because his primary impetus is the free-flow of unconscious mind. This means a personality of easy change from one thing to another which, although it makes him a good companion, may produce an irritating and unstable fickleness in a situation where the natural balance is strained. Under bad conditions this Prince may move from place to place, from person to person, and from job to job in search of an imaginary perfection which he can never achieve.

PRINCESS OF CUPS
THE AMBITIOUS DAUGHTER
Roots: *Hanged Man, Devil*
Sun in Cancer, Moon in Capricorn

An orderly young woman who manipulates without concern for others. Well-liked and successful, she is the ideal executive for a large group. She seems tough, but is actually vulnerable and sensitive. In this card the unconscious and the free flow of imagination turn toward the material world. Control in the material environment is the acting out of a dream. *The Princess of Cups*, who is very practical and ambitious, sets a clear course which will bring about what she has imagined for herself: wealth and power, the pinnacle of the material (Capricorn) condition. She is logical, an excellent business woman, though on the other hand she is not especially suited to family life. There is always a tension between the desire for things and the reality of them. The operative principle is that of expansive imagination versus solid absolute "reality." This princess ideally balances between the two, but not easily. She is never entirely comfortable because she can never completely realize her dreams. That is why she is ceaselessly ambitious. She is ever striving, ever working toward the realization of her ideals. In a reading this card should be understood to represent struggle between two very different principles and the constant attempt to bring mental pictures into something ultimately solid.

ACE OF CUPS
CHANGE OF FEELINGS
Roots: *Fool, Hanged Man*
Pluto in Cancer

The Root of Feelings. This is the most emotional card of the deck where feeling precedes thought or action. There is a powerful emotional upheaval in which new feelings are substituted for old. This may mean a change of feelings for another or a complete reversal of values such as turning to a new religion or political movement. In any event, a radical swing affects all levels. But since Pluto represents the masses, the greater society, *The Ace of Cups* is not generally a card of personal interaction. It may show a tremendous outpouring of group energy to effect change. However, the fact that change of feelings has been responsible for something new may not be obvious. This will be the correct interpretation if *The Ace of Cups* appears in the upper left cell of hidden thoughts and feelings.

TWO OF CUPS
ADVENTURE
Roots: *Magician, Hanged Man*
Uranus in Cancer

Experience which is quite out of the ordinary. Travel, new customs, brief sexual encounter. When the brilliant and intuitive mind of *The Magician* reaches water it stimulates a special flow of consciousness. Like a powerful wind across a lake, there is no telling where the waves may fall. Something new and interesting is certain to happen. The card refers to an experience which is totally out of the ordinary and which is not, necessarily, without some peril. This could mean danger, loss of security, as well as trouble at home or at work. There is no certainty with this card. *The Magician* and *The Hanged Man* is, under any circumstances, quite a combination!

THREE OF CUPS
SECURE ENVIRONMENT
Roots: *High Priestess, Hanged Man*
Neptune in Cancer

This is a card of the pleasures of "home," which can relate to the individual, to a family, or to the whole human race. It may show a creatively idealistic overview which strives to bring people together to produce a secure environment and to create understanding. The goals may be noble and there can be some very emotional fantasies connected with *The Three of Cups.* It can show significant personal sacrifice for a greater good and the comfort and safety in a domestic environment. Money and financial ease may come through the mother or her family. Badly placed, the card may suggest a completely unrealistic point of view about the home or group. It may also point to the results of extremes of pleasure such as obesity caused by overindulgence, hangovers, or becoming jaded and bored by constant stimulation.

FOUR OF CUPS
PLEASURE
Roots: *Wheel of Fortune, Hanged Man*
Jupiter in Cancer

This card means comfort, charity, kindness and good humor. It signifies amusing companionship, parties, dinners, and extremes of pleasure. When the planet of good fortune enters the sign of Cardinal Water it emphasizes beauty, sharing, and good feelings. It is understood that at one level water represents personal feelings, but that at another and more profound level it is the unconscious. So the card can represent either the pleasure of interaction with others, or it can mean an inner peace, the successful achievement of the meditative condition illustrated by the man hanging in space.

FIVE OF CUPS
TROUBLES
Roots: *Tower, Hanged Man*
Mars in Cancer

This card shows the most difficult and painful of human experiences which are (as opposed to *The Ten of Cups*) of one's own making. Could a reader ask for a better definition of disaster than these two cards side by side? Lingering and incurable illness, ill-will, lies, slander, and theft are suggested. There may be a scandal of the worst kind and events creating great indecision about what to do. Self-determination is lost; a person becomes subject to the influence and whims of others. There is a risk of drowning, scalding, or poisons in food. All of this may be the result of an unconscious and masochistic desire for negative experience (punishment?), which could perhaps be indicated if *The Five of Cups* appears in the upper left cell of the spread.

SIX OF CUPS
SYMPATHETIC ATTACHMENT
Roots: *Sun, Hanged Man*
Sun in Cancer

Selfless care for family and group; the individual is submerged in the collective mind. This is an extremely complex card where, for good or bad, the group assumes more importance than the individual. The person's self-perception is primarily in terms of service to a group. This card may show a phase, like that of teens needing peer support. And as the individual is submerged in the collective mind, self-reliance may disappear and be replaced by reliance on that group. There is a very strong attachment to external things, to people and to possessions, which, if selfless dedication, may be very positive. At an extreme, there may be moodiness and withdrawal from needed friends. Or there may be some other serious problem. Under any circumstances, the card shows a potential for masochistic behavior.

SEVEN OF CUPS
OBSTACLES
Roots: *Empress, Hanged Man*
Venus in Cancer

Obstacles, primarily to love and money, may be subtle and may involve one or both parents. There may be family strife—a parent may try to impede a relationship, or there may be a serious clash as father and mother attempt to control values. *The Seven of Cups* may show needs, a search for the security of a warm and loving material environment. This may show transition, an overcoming of obstacles with effort. It may also be a card of sacrifice.

EIGHT OF CUPS
CHANGEABILITY
Roots: *Chariot, Hanged Man*
Mercury in Cancer

The Eight of Cups may show relationships that are short-lived. There are many superficial pursuits and amusing pastimes, such as dancing and music which captivate briefly. Feeling and intuition are more important than thinking. Here is a dilettante with a grasp of many subjects but with little mastery in any area. The card indicates a very immature personality unable to make permanent commitments. Relationships are short-lived with partners, but are profitable with societies and associations. There are many superficial pursuits, some of which succeed.

NINE OF CUPS
VACILLATION
Roots: *Moon, Hanged Man*
Moon in Cancer

This card shows a free flow of ideas, thoughts, and emotions which may be positive or negative. The nature of control needs to be determined: if controlled by others, there is a terrible uncertainty, an inability to focus, and a sense of purposelessness. If self-controlled, this flow can be very powerful. It may describe an intentional diminishing of personality-focus and loosening of the bonds of "reality." Water and Mother are very important here. (It is said that "The Mother teaches the Son to meditate.")

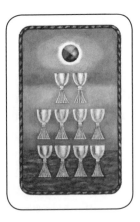

TEN OF CUPS
PAIN AND SORROW
Roots: *World, Hanged Man*
Saturn in Cancer

A terrible card meaning the end of a cycle, divorce, banishment, loss of profession, sickness, and perhaps death. This card is generally one of great pain and sorrow. The weight of the world, the apparent security and certainty of the material condition, is shaken to the core. A primary structure of one's life is destroyed. In a reading *The Ten of Cups* is occasionally "neutralized" by being next to a very good card such as *The Wheel of Fortune*.

SWORDS
(AIR, FAMILY OF JUSTICE)

Slowed down by Pentacles (Earth)
Increased by Wands (Fire)
Works with Cups (Water)

KING OF SWORDS
THE ROMANTIC FATHER
Roots: *Justice, Emperor*
Sun in Libra, Moon in Aries

This King is a strong-willed, active and independen man who loves change and is often drawn to the eccentric and the bizarre. He is gregarious, but is sometimes aloof and withdrawn and can be very thoughtless, even cruel—acting without concern for the feelings of others. He is a highly intelligent and romantically-creative person who tends to be outgoing and flamboyant but who, although he expends a great deal of energy is, under the surface, far more thoughtful and self-controlled than most realize. In this King of Air, the Libran balancing of the Scales of *Justice* prevails over the fire of Aries. His mind is in command over the more passionate dynamic qualities. And insofar as his reason stands behind physical power, he is an excellent athlete. He understands that he has a great deal of control, both physically and mentally and usually does what he wants to do. He does not easily suffer having others impede his freedom to be creative and independent. He sets high standards for himself and expects a great deal from those around him. But few can quite reach his romantic expectations.

QUEEN OF SWORDS
THE DIPLOMATIC MOTHER
Roots: *Justice*, *Hanged Man*
Sun in Libra, Moon in Cancer

The Queen of Swords is a delightful woman who is perceptive, sensitive and flexible. She goes to great lengths to avoid confrontation (which tends to create anxiety for her) but is ferocious when wronged. Although she has little interest in social causes or civil rights, and can be deceitful and disingenuous, *The Queen of Swords* is a remarkably sensitive and perceptive person who is alert to the feelings of others and who never wants to offend. She is very flexible and adapts easily to new situations and demands. But, on the negative side, her desire to please may be so great that she deals with people in a very shallow way. Her personality is somewhat ambiguous for, although she is quite ambitious and tends to seek a public spotlight, she draws her strength from the security of family and home, which she will defend like a mother lioness. She is capable of great cunning and ruthlessness to get what she wants. But the selfish, demanding, and potentially cruel aspects of her personality are rarely seen by others. *The Queen of Swords* is almost like two people. There is the charming and agreeable Persona, and there is the inner person who is highly self-protective and manipulative.

PRINCE OF SWORDS
THE IDEALISTIC SON
Roots: *Justice*
Sun in Libra, Moon in Libra

This is a young man who is graceful and charming. He loves to love and escapes the coarse world in storybook fantasies. A wonderful companion. He is kind, intelligent and gentle, but is quite gullible. *The Prince of Swords* is a very sensitive, attractive, and self-centered young man who lives in a mental world and loves to escape into fantasy. He seeks out beauty and harmony and dislikes anything which is disconsonant with the perfection of his inner vision. At best he is a nice and courteous person, happy, well-balanced, and well-liked by everyone. And although this prince often thinks about helping others in some way, he may be better at the planning than at the doing. Under bad circumstances he may be trapped in his own fantasy world, possibly becoming mentally ill and losing touch with reality. He is a dreamer by definition and whether or not he is able to accomplish anything substantive, to bring his dreams into reality, depends considerably upon those around him. With an ideal family, work environment, or marriage partner, the best qualities of wit, of intelligence, and of creativity, will be expressed by *The Prince of Swords*.

PRINCESS OF SWORDS
THE CONTROLLING DAUGHTER
Roots: *Justice, Devil*

Sun in Libra, Moon in Capricorn

This Princess is an orderly young woman whose feelings are under control. She is successful and well-liked, a shrewd manager who gets what she wants, believing that the end justifies the means. She projects arrogance and toughness, but this is self-protective. For this young woman everything must be perfectly organized. Her world is one of neat categories, which tends to make her good in business but, sometimes, an extremely ruthless and cold-blooded manager of people. Although she projects considerable charm and style as she goes about her work and is credited by associates as being effective and likeable, she is inwardly selfish and controlling. At her best the Princess is a positive organizer, one who contributes a creative overview. At her worst she is totally self-centered.

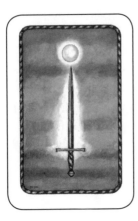

ACE OF SWORDS
CONFLICT OF IDEAS
Roots: *Fool, Justice*

Pluto in Libra

The *Ace of Swords* is the very root of thought. It means a raw power struggle, and ideological conflict where the strongest, not necessarily the best, wins. A great force exposes shocking secrets; the real truth comes out in a fight. This is a very direct and open fight (there is nothing subtle about it) in which somebody may be seriously hurt—physically, emotionally, and financially. Something positive and new may emerge as the outworn at home, at work, or in the nation, is discarded. But, again, the strongest is the winner.

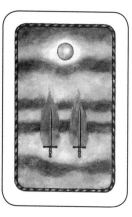

TWO OF SWORDS
OPPOSITION AND LOSS
Roots: *Magician, Justice*
Uranus in Libra

There is rivalry, opposition, criticism resulting in the absolute end of something. There is no possibility of return or resolution of a problem. A marriage ends, a friendship is destroyed, a spouse dies, a job is lost, a partnership or business relationship is ended. A person may be fired and the position given to somebody else. There may be financial loss through ill-considered speculation and a breach of relations with persons or organizations involved. Or there may be a collapse, verdict, or loss as the inevitable result of impulsive action. But readers may be surprised to learn that, on the other hand, in painting, literature, and music, this card is quite favorable and means increased imagination and intuition.

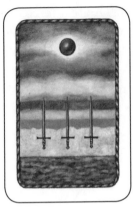

THREE OF SWORDS
IDEALISM
Roots: *High Priestess, Justice*
Neptune in Libra

This card signifies an idealistic and totally unrealistic approach to society and to personal relationships. There is a rejection of planned programs, a revolt against institutional structures, and a search for new and untried paths. This pioneering and creative imagination means success in an artistic endeavor if the person is disciplined to "ground" new ideas. But a lack of focus and emotional approach may mean real trouble in business and finance. The idealism can be one of self-deception about the importance of a relationship. It may also signal a sexual attraction or a brief infatuation. However, like the artist who is able to ground something new, in a serious love or friendship the idealism of *The Three of Swords* is usually positive.

FOUR OF SWORDS
IMAGINATION
Roots: *Wheel of Fortune, Justice*
Jupiter in Libra

Since imagination is the key to human progress, the energies of this card are among the most positive in the deck. It is this creative vision, in which the mind touches upon an inner "other," that carries civilization forward in arts, sciences, politics, etc. The person in question is very attractive to others; there are good feelings and caring friendships. This is also a card of mysticism and of religious feelings as a source of one's imagination which is a secret to others. At the most profound this is a magical journey into the unconscious bringing back ideas and images which can affect daily life. At the most mundane it can mean simply a good and safe journey. In some cases *The Four of Swords* can mean a secret treachery or a rather negative fluidity of ideas producing an inability to focus.

FIVE OF SWORDS
RASH DECISION
Roots: *Tower, Justice*
Mars in Libra

This can mean unconsidered action, a rapid choice, a decision reached with little hesitation. Feelings are more important than thought and one acts on an intuition, or a suspicion, that a certain course is appropriate. There could be a powerful sexual involvement, intense love, a hasty marriage or some other binding commitment made very rapidly—such as an expensive purchase or a partnership hurriedly formed, or a contract hastily drawn and signed. In a tarot spread *The Five of Swords* can signal something very perilous and unfair. What, after all can be more dangerous than *Justice* thrown off balance? The results of a rash decision could be disastrous. Under the worst of conditions the card can mean broken promises or contracts, and even the death of a partner or friend.

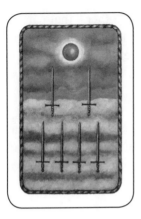

SIX OF SWORDS
JUSTICE
Roots: *Justice*
Sun in Libra

Justice is a very intellectual card. It shows harmony, justice, compassion, wisdom, as well as compromise and reconciliation of opposites. If a real lawsuit is involved, that action will be resolved with fairness. At a philosophical level it is the subjective correlate of the perfect and universal justice shown by the two tarot keys of *The Sun* and *Justice* (Libra) operating together. When *Justice* is perfected by *The Sun*, it means an objective justice which is" handed down" either from a court of law or from above. *The Six of Swords* may mean a person's attempt to do the right thing in a given situation, or it may mean striving to reach some inner balance.

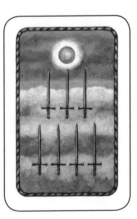

SEVEN OF SWORDS
LOVE
Roots: *Empress, Justice*
Venus in Libra

This shows almost perfect happiness, love and marriage, an ideal union, an intense and understanding friendship. All needs, physical and emotional, are met. The person is quite popular. Sociability and money is assured, perhaps through marriage or through a partner. A partnership in business will be very special and successful. This card represents the realization of complete happiness and joy, harmony and integration, as opposed to *The Seven of Wands* (Passion), where nothing can be pinned down. This card is so positive that the worst that can happen, under the most disastrous of circumstances, is that the harmony is somewhat diminished.

EIGHT OF SWORDS
INTELLECTUAL SKILL
Roots: *Chariot, Justice*
Mercury in Libra

Accomplished writing and scholarship, clear thought and creative inspiration are the attributes of *The Eight of Swords*. There is an effortless use of language, of research, and of plot. Communication is with clarity and flair and there is a great pleasure in dealing with ideas. Money comes through popular publications. There is also an excellent manipulation of business concepts. An approach which is both clear-sighted and inventive receives strong support from partner or colleagues. A person moves up very quickly in a company. The card is almost always quite good, but under bad influence it may show vacillation, delay, or an inability to choose a definite course of action.

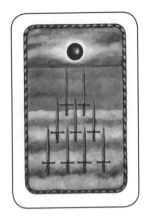

NINE OF SWORDS
SHARING
Roots: *Moon, Justice*
Moon in Libra

Here is shown good natured coop- eration, generosity, and sharing of daily activities. One person anticipates and provides for the needs of the other. Business partners mesh well. Relationships are carried on with refinement and charm. The worst that can happen is that one partner becomes selfish and throws off the balance.

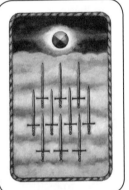

TEN OF SWORDS
GAIN THROUGH PARTNERSHIP
Roots: *World, Justice*
Saturn in Libra

Success comes with people working together. The partners in marriage or in business may be very different, but they are a perfect and productive match. Hard work and long hours together pay off in a productive marriage, an elegant refined home, or a comfortable and profitable business. With bad influences partners may disagree and challenge each other producing disloyalty, diminished profits, and bad feelings.

PENTACLES
(EARTH, FAMILY OF THE DEVIL)

Slowed down by Swords (Air)
Increased by Cups (Water)
Works with Wands (Fire)

KING OF PENTACLES
THE RESPONSIBLE FATHER
Roots: *Devil, Emperor*
Sun in Capricorn, Moon in Aries

The Root of Matter. This is an independent, assertive and uncompromising man who believes that he is always right. He has a keen intellect but is completely materialistic, having no interest in religion or philosophy. He can be a harsh and unbending person, one who is easily annoyed and who may often create difficult and tense situations at home and in the workplace. He is a strong leader who must be at the head of everything in which he is involved, a very hard worker who makes great demands upon himself as well as upon those around him. His need to assume responsibilities makes him ideally suited to lead a large corporation or to hold an important government position. He might be a military officer. Or, if influenced positively by *The Chariot* (Mercury), he might have the keen intellect of a scientist or of a philosopher. On the other hand, if negatively aspected in a tarot spread this King may be a very harsh and unbending person.

71

QUEEN OF PENTACLES
THE SECRETIVE MOTHER
Roots: Devil, Hanged Man
Sun in Capricorn, Moon in Cancer

The Queen of Pentacles is a woman who is economical to an extreme. She seeks business success, believing that wealth and power justify whatever means are necessary to achieve them. A deeply private person, she never wants people to know what she is thinking and is very secretive about her personal life and profession. She has deep insecurities—almost to the point of borderline paranoia and is torn between practical things and feelings. Where money is involved this materialistic and possessive Queen is cautious and economical. She wants to be in control of her own fortunes and is an achiever-type personality who feels good when she brings organization to a situation. She may, in fact, become a very prominent public figure. Or, being natively rather materialistic and possessive, she may apply her skills in budgeting and arranging schedules or creating an excellent home environment for her family. But if this Queen is badly aspected with other cards, she is likely to be borderline paranoid, extremely miserly, selfish, and overbearing. Money and possessions may assume almost pathological significance. And rather than earning respect and attention, she demands it.

PRINCE OF PENTACLES
THE SELF-ASSURED SON
Roots: *Devil, Justice*
Sun in Capricorn, Moon in Libra

The Prince of Pentacles, who is popular and well-liked, achieves through the force of his personality. He can be gentle and caring despite a tendency to detachment and impatience, but does not easily admit his own fault and sees others as responsible for his problems. This independent, self-controlled young man approaches everything from a rational point of view. He tends to be quiet and reserved, keeping his feelings to himself and, in a work situation, doing a very careful and thorough job. His behavior may vary according to outside influences. He will, for example, be generous if affected by Jupiter, active if affected by Mars, or intellectual if affected by Mercury. So the rulerships and relationships of the cards around *The Prince of Pentacles* are of special importance. Under bad aspects his moodiness and suspiciousness may bring about some very unfortunate situations. In the worst case, he may become withdrawn to the point of mental illness.

PRINCESS OF PENTACLES
THE ISOLATED DAUGHTER
Roots: *Devil*
Sun in Capricorn, Moon in Capricorn

The *Princess of Pentacles* is a loner who has almost no friends. She is competent, tactful, and self-controlled, but has never learned the social skills of communicating personal feelings. Her judgment is polar. *The Princess of Pentacles* has little tolerance for ambiguity and wants everything to be clearly defined. She is a thoughtful, quiet, and steady person, but can be too independent for her own good, and may thus set herself apart from others, or she may actually wish to be alone. She does not tend to feel things very strongly and is primarily focused on herself and on her own problems. In fact, she is self-controlled almost to an extreme, not easily letting people know what she thinks or who she really is. But with friends this quality translates into her being very trustworthy with secrets. Moreover, being natively methodical and cautious, she is quite good in business, and may be a very strong and reliable manager. This is one tarot personality which may vary considerably according to planetary influences. In the presence of *The Tower* (Mars), or *The Wheel of Fortune* (Jupiter) she may be very aggressive and ambitious. Contact with *The Chariot* (Mercury) may make her very intellectual.

ACE OF PENTACLES
SECURITY DESTROYED
Roots: *Fool, Devil*
Pluto in Capricorn

Here is the root of all matter and the principle that matter is self-renewing. The card indicates a revolution in the material world, dependable structures utterly destroyed and cleared away. This could mean urban renewal or it could be a revolution which brings down a government. It is, in any case, a traumatic event which is followed by uncertainty about what is going to happen next. In the presence of *The Ace of Pentacles* the dust has not settled. In business this may mean ruin and bankruptcy; collapse of an institution .

TWO OF PENTACLES
REORGANIZATION
Roots: *Magician, Devil*
Uranus in Capricorn

The *Two of Pentacles* shows a highly original and organized restructuring. A thoughtful and intelligently administered change which is a product of ambition and individual genius. A leader of great vision challenges accepted authority; outworn structures are swiftly replaced as the result of long planning. No values are implied here; what emerges is not necessarily better. Negatively, the challenge to structure may produce bad feelings, public criticism, and censure from superiors.

THREE OF PENTACLES
RESPONSE TO CONFLICT
Roots: *High Priestess, Devil*
Neptune in Capricorn

Conflicts bring about changes of social structure in a home or work situation. There may have been early family problems, especially with the father, later producing a painful and distressing encounter with repressed materials of childhood which affects daily life. There is a very eccentric and ambivalent attitude toward authority figures. A strong employer may, for example, be viewed as like the father to whom one became hostile early in life. However, since the confrontations of this card are dark and internal, the form of response to conflict may be unclear. On a positive note, *The Three of Pentacles* can mean success in art, music, and philosophy, all of which delve into the unconscious and bring materials "down" into the world of structure.

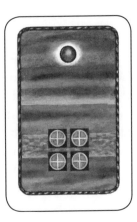

FOUR OF PENTACLES
WEALTH
Roots: *Wheel of Fortune, Devil*
Jupiter in Capricorn

Old money and enormous financial resources are shown here. Much money, possibly inherited, is managed with care, frugality, and understanding of its value. There is a very serious, humorless, approach to vast personal resources. Money is not an end in itself; what is important is the process of dealing with money, and maintaining a lifestyle. Success in an executive career or in management of large financial resources and people is assured. The person is liked by subordinates, who are always ready to help. Everything works perfectly as achievement and prosperity flow in. This card may, parenthetically, represent an unorthodox approach to religion and, under negative influences, the good fortune may become so extreme that there is overindulgence.

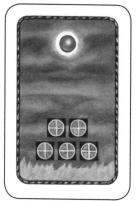

FIVE OF PENTACLES
RESPONSIBLE AUTHORITY
Roots: *Tower, Devil*
Mars in Capricorn

The *Five of Pentacles* shows an ambitious person who has earned prominence through hard work and willingness to accept responsibility. Pursuit of money is very important and an initial inheritance may have made possible an executive position. Business runs smoothly; the family is comfortable and well provided for. However, the person's tendency to impatience and irritability may bring conflict with co-workers, especially superiors. There may be friction with parents or brothers and sisters, although this is usually minor. In any event, assertive behavior can cause criticism and jealousy. Resentment can cause irreconcilable differences resulting in separation, firing, divorce, or even death.

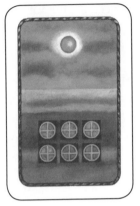

SIX OF PENTACLES
WEALTH THROUGH HARD WORK
Roots: *Sun, Devil*
Sun in Capricorn

L ong and hard work, with unswerving self-discipline, brings wealth and power. This is a solitary road where an extrovert under absolute self-control works against odds and opposition with great patience and perserverence. Although there are dark periods of uncertainty and depression, self-assurance guarantees eventual success. Clarity in communication is essential. The person, whose motto is "time is money," may inspire many people. However, *The Six of Pentacles* individual may be seen as cold and overly strict, placing money, power, and success ahead of people and their feelings

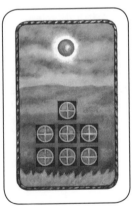

SEVEN OF PENTACLES
GAIN THROUGH COMMERCE
Roots: *Empress, Devil*
Venus in Capricorn

T his is a powerful card of certain financial reward through business investments, stocks, or banking.

Money and reward are pursued to the exclusion of all else. The card may signify a person of genius for business management, a master of guile and manipulation whose friends and family are merely pawns in the process and are, essentially, expendable. But under bad influences the card may signify a marriage or friendship destroyed in a struggle between ambition at work and the emotional demands of friends and family. Business may also serve as an emotional escape from friends and family.

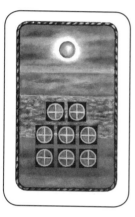

EIGHT OF PENTACLES
MANIPULATION AND SECRETS
Roots: *Chariot, Devil*
Mercury in Capricorn

The Eight of Pentacles is a card of mystery, of intrigue, of spying, and of secret plans. Subtlety and diplomacy are applied to some specific end. Great intelligence and seriousness create a very detailed presentation which appears complete and accurate, but which is really a cover for secret ideas. People are manipulated secretly and the agenda is hidden. There are agreements in private, considerations and negotiations which are not obvious, and in the plan attention to detail is essential. Under certain circumstances this could mean academic honors or a very important position. The sub-rosa activity is neither good nor bad. But negative possibilities include mail delayed and communications held up.

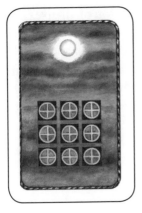

NINE OF PENTACLES
SELFISHNESS
Roots: *Moon, Devil*
Moon in Capricorn

Here is a person in egocentric control with no concern whatsoever for the feelings of others. There is calculation for personal gain which may be good or bad. But overall, this is an anti-social card where everything revolves around a person's satisfying needs. The person is a complete center of attention who flaunts social conventions by which others abide. At best a reward is earned, and this could mean favors and popularity. But at worst, this could mean destructiveness, ruthlessness, notorious scandal, personal attacks, and a loss of reputation.

TEN OF PENTACLES
ISOLATED POWER
Roots: *World, Devil*
Saturn in Capricorn

One is isolated in winning and in having to maintain power and wealth. A person finds nothing more important than position, money, and power and finds little in common with subordinates. Ambitions are structured. There is a studied directness, a certain roughness which many find disarming. Scrooge is separated from others as he spends all of his time counting his money and planning to make more. Isolation at the top means loneliness. The card may show strength hiding insecurity and, if it is badly placed, there may be a personal downfall, a devastating loss of money and profession.

Rationale for the Assignment
of Attributions to the Tarot

(First section reprinted from *Tarot Psychology,*
Volume I of *The Jungian Tarot Trilogy*)

It is clear today that some of the most commonly accepted ideas about tarot, especially those of late nineteenth century French and English occultists, were an arbitrary attempt to create a "secret tradition" in tarot where, as history demonstrates, none actually existed.

One who seeks a comprehensive scheme underlying the many charts and tables of attributions bequeathed by writers of that era is inevitably disappointed, or is simply frustrated by the attempt. In light of close scrutiny, a great deal of tarot interpretation from *La Belle Époque* is discovered to be confusing, internally inconsistent, and reflective of the writer's own personal perspective.

Thus one may legitimately seek a plan of attributions which is in agreement with the broadest aspects of the Western Mystery Tradition. The present scheme cannot be considered original or innovative. It is, rather, a conservative effort to relate the tarot cards to an interpretive school at least two thousand years more ancient than the cards themselves.

In this regard, it should be emphasized that although the Jungian Tarot deck has been created primarily for meditation, it may be used as is any standard deck. Many people enjoy divination with the cards, a practice which has been said to promote the development of intuition and psychism. Certainly the tarot has been so linked to "fortune telling" in the past that the issue of divination must be addressed. And indeed, despite the fact that precise measurement of results is currently impossible, frequent readers of tarot cards using this method report that they have achieved some remarkably accurate predictions. If such is the case, it may be found that the Jungian Tarot deck, emphasizing the archetypes of the collective unconscious, produces better results than other decks. The system proposed here relates card meanings to The Tree of Life—and to Planets in Houses—in such a way that anyone well grounded in both will know the meaning of a card in question without further study.

The Minor Arcana and Court Cards

Through this system of attributions, serious students of astrology, many of whom may have considered the tarot to be separate and distinct from their interests, will find a new world of symbolism in their immediate grasp. In fact, those who are already conversant with the nuances of astrology may find that they understand the tarot better than many who have devoted years of attention to the memorization of arbitrary tables of "meanings."

Involved also is the attribution of ten planets to the Tree of Life (see pages 89-90). In Kabbalistic terms, Pluto relates to Kether; Uranus relates to Chokmah; Neptune relates to Binah; and Saturn relates to Malkuth. This allows ten specific planets with which to deal and to which values are easily assigned: One can specify a planet in a suit through a Cardinal sign, i.e., the root of Fire, Aries (Wands), the root of Water, Cancer (Cups), the root of Air, Libra (Swords), and the root of Earth, Capricorn (Pentacles). This is extremely simple:

Aces = Pluto	Eights = Mercury
Twos = Uranus	Nines = Moon
Threes = Neptune	Tens = Saturn
Fours = Jupiter	Wands = Aries
Fives = Mars	Cups = Cancer
Sixes = Sun	Swords = Libra
Sevens = Venus	Pentacles = Capricorn

So *The Ace of Wands* means Pluto in Aries. *The Ace of Cups* means Pluto in Cancer. *The Ace of Swords* means Pluto in Libra. *The Ace of Pentacles* means Pluto in Capricorn.

The plan for the Court Cards is equally direct. Personalities are defined according to the placement of Sun and Moon in a natal chart. Since all of the Wands are Aries, *The King of Wands* has the personality of a man with the Sun in Aries and the Moon in Aries. His is the personality of pure fire. *The Queen of Wands* has a personality with the Sun in Aries and the Moon in Cancer. Hers is a fiery personality tempered by Water. Generally this system tends to describe more specific human qualities, and perhaps more human frailties, then the idealized schemes of the past.

Certainly, there are a few surprises when the Minor Cards are attributed in this way. A good example is *The Five of Wands*, which has been called "Strife." But when *The Five of Wands* is related to Mars in Aries, it is seen to be a card of tremendous creative energy, of originality, and of courage. It is a card of independence, of success, of popularity, and of outgoing force which may be rapidly expended.

As another example one may cite *The Three of Swords* earlier considered to be a card of pain and sorrow. But as Neptune in Libra, the positive house of Venus, it becomes a card of art, of poetry, of refinement. It is a card of love, of friendship and of good fortune. It is the flowing Neptunian force expressed through thought (Air/Swords).

These two cards, especially, are mentioned to underscore the fact that to relate the tarot to the mainstream of Western esoteric thought requires that we discard some deeply-ingrained notions.

The Astrological configurations on the basis of which the cards are explained in this book are as follows:

84

SUMMARY OF CONTEMPORARY TAROT ASTROLOGY

Attributions of Signs and Planets to the Kabbalistic Tree of Life as shown in the next section.

FOOL
Pluto/The Aces
Rules: Scorpio *(Death)*

MAGICIAN
Uranus/The Twos/The Kings
Rules: Aquarius *(Star)*

HIGH PRIESTESS
**Neptune/The Threes/
The Queens**
Rules: Pisces *(Judgment)*

EMPRESS
Venus/The Sevens
Rules: Taurus *(Hierophant)*
and Libra *(Justice)*

EMPEROR
Aries
Ruled by: Mars *(Tower)*

HIEROPHANT
Taurus
Ruled by: Venus *(Empress)*

LOVER
Gemini
Ruled by: Mercury *(Chariot)*

CHARIOT
Mercury/The Eights
Rules: Gemini *(Lover)*
and Virgo *(Hermit)*

STRENGTH
Leo
Ruled by: The Sun *(Sun)*

HERMIT
Virgo
Ruled by: Mercury *(Chariot)*

WHEEL OF FORTUNE
Jupiter/The Fours
Rules: Gemini *(Lover)*

JUSTICE
Libra
Ruled by: Venus *(Empress)*

HANGED MAN
Cancer
Ruled by: Moon *(Moon)*

DEATH
Scorpio
Ruled by: Pluto *(Fool)*

TEMPERANCE
Sagittarius
Ruled by: Jupiter *(Wheel of Fortune)*

DEVIL
Capricorn
Ruled by: Saturn *(World)*

TOWER
Mars/The Fives
Rules: Aries *(Emperor)*

THE STAR
Aquarius
Ruled by: Uranus *(Magician)*

THE MOON
The Moon/The Nines
Rules: Cancer *(Hanged Man)*

THE SUN
The Sun/The Sixes/
The Princes
Rules: Leo *(Strength)*

JUDGMENT
Pisces
Ruled by: Neptune
(High Priestess)

THE WORLD
Saturn/The Tens/
The Princesses
Rules: Capricorn *(Devil)*

WANDS

KING OF WANDS
Sun in Aries
Moon in Aries
(Emperor)

QUEEN OF WANDS
Sun in Aries
Moon in Cancer
(Emperor/Hanged Man)

PRINCE OF WANDS
Sun in Aries
Moon in Libra
(Emperor/Justice)

PRINCESS OF WANDS
Sun in Aries
Moon in Capricorn
(Emperor/Devil)

ACE OF WANDS
Pluto in Aries
(Fool/Emperor)

TWO OF WANDS
Uranus in Aries
(Magician/Emperor)

THREE OF WANDS
Neptune in Aries
(High Priestess/Emperor)

FOUR OF WANDS
Jupiter in Aries
(Wheel of Fortune/
Emperor)

FIVE OF WANDS
Mars in Aries
(Tower/Emperor)

SIX OF WANDS
Sun in Aries
(Sun/Emperor)

SEVEN OF WANDS
Venus in Aries
(Empress/Emperor)

EIGHT OF WANDS
Mercury in Aries
(Chariot/Emperor)

NINE OF WANDS
Moon in Aries
(Moon/Emperor)

TEN OF WANDS
Saturn in Aries
(World/Emperor)

CUPS

KING OF CUPS
Sun in Cancer
Moon in Aries
(Hanged Man/Emperor)

QUEEN OF CUPS
Sun in Cancer
Moon in Cancer
(Hanged Man)

PRINCE OF CUPS
Sun in Cancer
Moon in Libra
(Hanged Man/Justice)

PRINCESS OF CUPS
Sun in Cancer
Moon in Capricorn
(Hanged Man/Devil)

ACE OF CUPS
Pluto in Cancer
(Fool/Hanged Man)

TWO OF CUPS
Uranus in Cancer
(Magician/Hanged Man)

THREE OF CUPS
Neptune in Cancer
(High Priestess/Hanged Man)

FOUR OF CUPS
Jupiter in Cancer
(Wheel of Fortune/Hanged Man)

FIVE OF CUPS
Mars in Cancer
(Tower/Hanged Man)

SIX OF CUPS
Sun in Cancer
(Sun/Hanged Man)

SEVEN OF CUPS
Venus in Cancer
(Empress/Hanged Man)

EIGHT OF CUPS
Mercury in Cancer
(Chariot/Hanged Man)

NINE OF CUPS
Moon in Cancer
(Moon/Hanged Man)

TEN OF CUPS
Saturn in Cancer
(World/Hanged Man)

SWORDS

KING OF SWORDS
Sun in Libra
Moon in Aries
(Justice/Emperor)

QUEEN OF SWORDS
Sun in Libra
Moon in Cancer
(Justice/Hanged Man)

PRINCE OF SWORDS
Sun in Libra
Moon in Libra
(Justice)

PRINCESS OF SWORDS
Sun in Libra
Moon in Capricorn
(Justice/Devil)

ACE OF SWORDS
Pluto in Libra
(Fool/Justice)

TWO OF SWORDS
Uranus in Libra
(Magician/Justice)

THREE OF SWORDS
Neptune in Libra
(High Priestess/Justice)

FOUR OF SWORDS
Jupiter in Libra
(Wheel of Fortune/Justice)

FIVE OF SWORDS
Mars in Libra
(Tower/Justice)

SIX OF SWORDS
Sun in Libra
(Sun/Justice)

SEVEN OF SWORDS
Venus in Libra
(Empress/Justice)

EIGHT OF SWORDS
Mercury in Libra
(Chariot/Justice)

NINE OF SWORDS
Moon in Libra
(Moon/Justice)

TEN OF SWORDS
Saturn in Libra
(World/Justice)

PENTACLES

KING OF PENTACLES
Sun in Capricorn
Moon in Aries
(Devil/Emperor)

QUEEN OF PENTACLES
Sun in Capricorn
Moon in Cancer
(Devil/Hanged Man)

PRINCE OF PENTACLES
Sun in Capricorn
Moon in Libra
(Devil/Justice)

PRINCESS OF PENTACLES
Sun in Capricorn
Moon in Capricorn
(Devil)

ACE OF PENTACLES
Pluto in Capricorn
(Fool/Devil)

TWO OF PENTACLES
Uranus in Capricorn
(Magician/ Devil)

THREE OF PENTACLES
Neptune in Capricorn
(High Priestess/Devil)

FOUR OF PENTACLES
Jupiter in Capricorn
(Wheel of Fortune/Devil)

FIVE OF PENTACLES
Mars in Capricorn
(Tower/Devil)

SIX OF PENTACLES
Sun in Capricorn
(Sun/Devil)

SEVEN OF PENTACLES
Venus in Capricorn
(Empress/Devil)

EIGHT OF PENTACLES
Mercury in Capricorn
(Chariot/Devil)

NINE OF PENTACLES
Moon in Capricorn
(Moon/Devil)

TEN OF PENTACLES
Saturn in Capricorn
(World/Devil)

KABBALAH

Kabbalah is a mystical system which grew out of early forms of Jewish mysticism and which assumed Christian elements over centuries, but to which all religions can be related. The key diagram of Kabbalah is the "Tree of Life," supposedly representing the entire universe. In this diagram circular centers of energy called *Sephiroth* are connected by lines called *Paths* which, according to Kabbalistic theory, represent different roads that the mystic travels in an inner universe. The highest path is that from which the universe evolves, and the lowest is the ground on which we walk. Attributions of Signs and of Planets are intended to express an interaction of balanced forces and the different experiences of the seeker of truth.

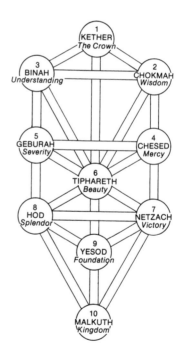

The Tree of Life

The system, which has evolved over many centuries, is quite complicated, although the basics of its attribution to tarot may be found in the following diagrams. Those who have not previously encountered this system may find it to be impossibly obtuse. However the essentials of tarot attribution to the Tree are given primarily so that there may be no question about the source of meanings assigned to the tarot cards. Pursuant to the most current understanding of tarot astrology Pluto, Uranus, and Neptune are appropriately included.

These diagrams will be of value as review to those who are already familiar with Kabbalistic symbolism. It is recommended that those for whom the system is new refer to *The Qabalistic Tarot: A Textbook of Mystical Philosophy* (Robert Wang, 2004).

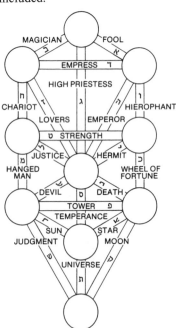

The Major Arcana on
the Tree of Life

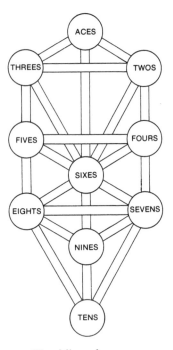

The Minor Arcana
on the Tree of Life

90

SOME USEFUL EXAMPLES
OF SPECIAL-CASE
TAROT MEANINGS

A very effective way in which some people teach astrology is by considering the unusual, asking, for example, what aspects would represent an automobile accident, or a rape, or some other disaster, or a condition not commonly seen. When this method is applied to the tarot, it tends to underscore some of the more exceptional meanings of the cards and helps a reader to see a range of possible interpretations of the same card under different circumstances. Following here are a few very specific examples of situations which the tarot can represent, including pathologies. As a general rule it can be said that the Major Arcana are objective forces, whereas the Minor Cards are subjective and are subject to the individual's perception. Many objective situations are caused by subjective conditions. This can mean an unconscious desire which brings the external (objective) energies into play.

As shown on page 4, *cards read either from right to left* (as in examples) or *left to right* according to placement on the board. The first card is the cause, and the second card is the effect.

Suicide
(Scorpio + Pluto)

A Head of
Government
(Aries + Sun)

Condition of
Delusion or Addiction
Caused by
Drugs or Alcohol
(Moon + Neptune)

Heart Attack
(Leo + Mars)

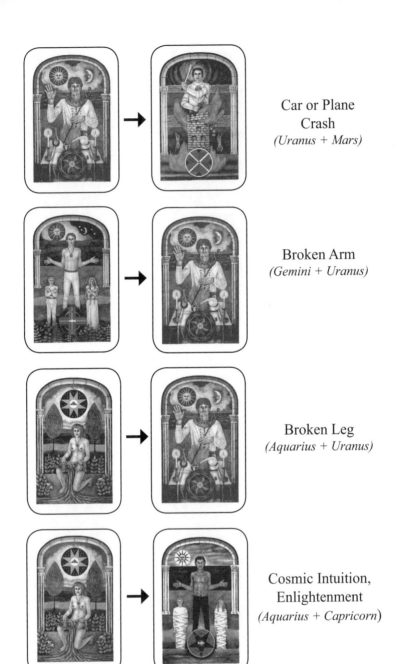

Car or Plane
Crash
(Uranus + Mars)

Broken Arm
(Gemini + Uranus)

Broken Leg
(Aquarius + Uranus)

Cosmic Intuition,
Enlightenment
(Aquarius + Capricorn)

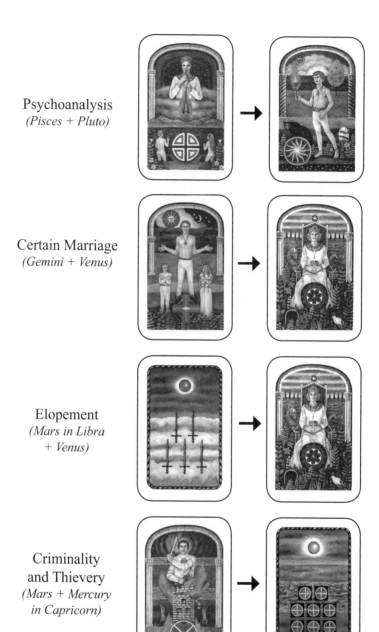

Psychoanalysis
(Pisces + Pluto)

Certain Marriage
(Gemini + Venus)

Elopement
*(Mars in Libra
+ Venus)*

Criminality
and Thievery
*(Mars + Mercury
in Capricorn)*

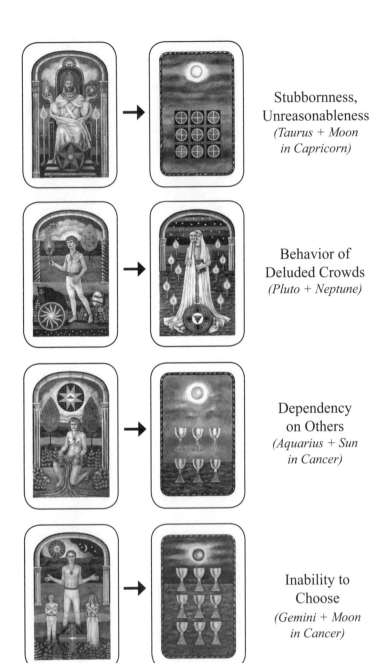

Stubbornness,
Unreasonableness
*(Taurus + Moon
in Capricorn)*

Behavior of
Deluded Crowds
(Pluto + Neptune)

Dependency
on Others
*(Aquarius + Sun
in Cancer)*

Inability to
Choose
*(Gemini + Moon
in Cancer)*

96

Self-Denial
(Pisces + Moon in Libra)

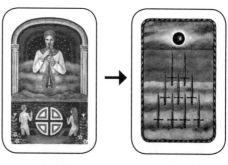

Anger and Irrationality
(Libra + Moon in Aries)

Education
(Mercury + Virgo)

Gossip
(Mercury + Moon in Capricorn)

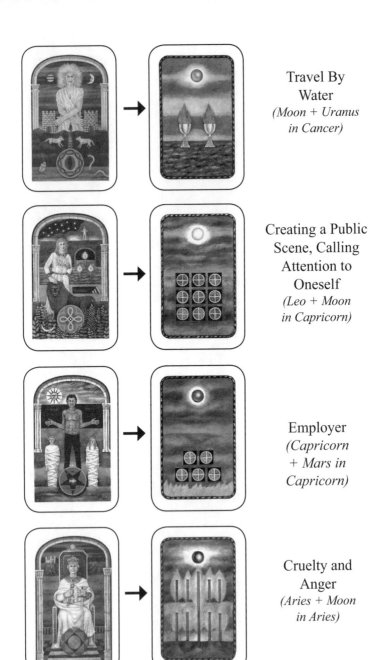

Travel By
Water
*(Moon + Uranus
in Cancer)*

Creating a Public
Scene, Calling
Attention to
Oneself
*(Leo + Moon
in Capricorn)*

Employer
*(Capricorn
+ Mars in
Capricorn)*

Cruelty and
Anger
*(Aries + Moon
in Aries)*

98

QUICK SUMMARY
OF MEANINGS

The Major Arcana

FOOL
Idea, Originality

MAGICIAN
Invention, Innovation

HIGH PRIESTESS
Fluctuation, Dreams

EMPRESS
Expansion, Fruitfulness

EMPEROR
Aggressive Power

CHARIOT
Communications, Reason

HIEROPHANT
Ruling Temporal Power

LOVER
Union of Opposites, Swiftness

STRENGTH
Strength, Creative Energy

HERMIT
Divine Inspiration, Guidance

WHEEL OF FORTUNE
Extravagance, Good Fortune

JUSTICE
Justice, Balance

HANGED MAN
Reversal, Psychism

DEATH
Transition, Healing, Sex

TEMPERANCE
Experiment, Trial, Combination

DEVIL
Material Force, Steadfastness

TOWER
Applied Energy, Sudden Force

STAR
Inspiration, Knowledge

MOON
Dark Dreams, Deception

SUN
Glory, Honor, Riches

JUDGMENT
Isolated Introspection

WORLD
Practical Matters, Materiality

101

The Minor Arcana

WANDS

K: Aggressive
Q: Stylish
P: Affectionate
Ps: Clever
A: Birth and Death
2: Invention
3: Fantasy
4: Success
5: Assertiveness
6: Strong Leaderhip
7: Passion
8: Literary Activity
9: Anger and Volatility
10: Control Over Others

SWORDS

K: Romantic
Q: Diplomatic
P: Idealistic
Ps: Controlling
A: Conflict of Ideas
2: Opposition and Loss
3: Idealism
4: Imagination
5: Rash Decision
6: Justice
7: Love
8: Intellectual Skill
9: Sharing
10: Gain thru Partnership

CUPS

K: Intellectual
Q: Emotional
P: Charming
Ps: Ambitious
A: Change of Feelings
2: Adventure
3: Secure Environment
4: Pleasure
5: Troubles
6: Sympathetic Attachment
7: Obstacles
8: Changeability
9: Vacillation
10: Pain and Sorrow

PENTACLES

K: Responsible
Q: Secretive
P: Self-Assured
Ps: Isolated
A: Security Destroyed
2: Reorganization
3: Response to Conflict
4: Wealth
5: Responsible Authority
6: Wealth Thru Hard Work
7: Gain Thru Commerce
8: Manipulation & Secrets
9: Selfishness
10: Isolated Power